HABITS OF GOODNESS

HABITS OF GOODNESS

CASE STUDIES IN THE

SOCIAL CURRICULUM

BY RUTH SIDNEY CHARNEY

With Case Studies by Six Elementary School Teachers

All net proceeds from the sale of *Habits of Goodness: Case Studies in the Social Curriculum* support the work of Northeast Foundation for Children, Inc., a nonprofit, educational foundation established to demonstrate through teaching, research, and consultation, a sensible and systematic approach to schooling.

The stories in this book are all based on real events in the classroom. However, in order to respect the privacy of students, names and many identifying characteristics of students and situations have been changed.

ISBN 0-9618636-5-x
Library of Congress catalog card number 97-065056

Second printing April 2000

Title page photograph: Peter Wrenn
Cover photograph, top: Cherry Wyman
Cover photograph, bottom: Peter Wrenn
Cover and book design: Rebecca S. Neimark, Twenty-Six Letters

Northeast Foundation for Children
71 Montague City Road
Greenfield, MA 01301
1-800-360-6332

TABLE OF CONTENTS

ACKNOWLEDGMENTS

I received so much help in the writing of this book. The teachers who agreed to explore the case study approach made it happen. I also owe much to the many teachers and writers who have inspired and taught me, many already mentioned in the text. But there are other colleagues and friends who have provided crucial conversations and support which allowed this manuscript to move from draft to draft to draft, as ideas and revisions were taking shape. This has truly been a collaborative endeavor.

Roxann Kriete has been my editor, mentor and co-author for this project. She has, from the start, shared the puzzles and excitements that so often turn muddle into meaning. I am deeply grateful for her intelligent and searching responses and for her very words, phrases and insightful revisions.

Nancy Ratner has also edited this text, offering her wonderful gifts of wordsmithing and clear prose. She was willing to meet and discuss on a regular basis, to share her own views, to listen and react with honesty and considered judgment.

I want to thank the many people who read drafts and offered important critiques: Jane Lazarre, Jay Lord, Paula Denton, Linda Prokopy, Pam Porter, and Mary Beth Forton. Thank you always, Janie, for your faith in me. Thank you, Mary Beth, for your ongoing struggle to give clarity to the meanderings of our stories.

And as always there are those people who share so much of their time, expertise, spirit and commitment to children. They are an essential part of the company I keep. To mention a few: Barbara Nophlin, Khary Lazarre-White, Ann and Reuel Kaighn and Darius Marder. Thank you, Doug Jenest, for a warm work place.

I would also like to thank the many teachers in Washington, DC who opened their classroom doors and hearts to help show that there are so many profound applications to teaching children to care. To name just a few: Maurice Sykes, Barbara Freeman, Pat Harris, Betsy Morrell, Joyce Love, Sandra Norried, Austine Fowler, Linda Harrison, Kathleen Thomas, Mary Duru, Stephanie Abney, Virginia Burnette and so many more.

I also thank Laurie Tash for her careful and painstaking work that turned disks and paper into manuscript.

This project was first conceived of and encouraged by Northeast Foundation for Children's Editorial Board. I particularly want to thank Sharon Dunn and Steve Finer for their endorsements and support.

I am appreciative and always thankful for the wonderful home ground of Greenfield Center School and its staff, for the dedication and inspiration, friendship and fun I continually find in our shared commitments.

Finally, I am deeply thankful to my own wondrous children (Daniel, Emma, Apple and Hannah) and to those children I am fortunate to teach. And I thank NEFC for letting me do what I most love to do.

"Monsters are out there and claiming children in record numbers. And so we must stand up and be visible heroes, fighting for our children. I want people to understand the crisis that our children face and I want people to act."
—Geoffrey Canada, *Fist Stick Knife Gun*

"So we intervene. We intervene perceptively and creatively, attributing the best possible motive, and offering our help and our example in caring."
—Nel Noddings, *Caring*

"The question is not, Is it possible to educate all children well? but rather, Do we want to do it badly enough?
. . . Schools embody the dreams we have for our children."
—Deborah Meier, *The Power of Their Ideas*

INTRODUCTION

"Habits of Goodness"

"Hospitality isn't unusual, something you choose to do or not, it's ordinary," her voice softened. "It's like sleeping so that you will be rested when you wake. It's like gathering wood so that you can have a fire when the snow comes. It's like making pemmican instead of eating all the meat immediately. Like listening to good advice."

—Michael Dorris, *Guests*

I want to begin by telling a story that I heard several years ago which helped shape and inspire this project. It started when my husband and I attended a convocation that had been organized by area churches in memory of the Holocaust; we did not know the featured speaker. We went dutifully. We left with a gift. It was the gift of this story. Here is the story as I best remember it.[1]

The speaker, Phillip Hallie, began softly, his voice easy with the flow of memory and of practice. He was born in Chicago, a punk kid who learned early to use his fists and liked using them. He enlisted at the start of World War II, a willing soldier. But working in intelligence, he felt himself change as the campaigns continued, overwhelmed by the very information he gathered in the course of duty: unimaginable atrocities; extermination camps; deliberate cruelties mass produced; an endless parade of man's inhumanity to man. He grew numb trying to steel himself against the horror. Then, one day, as he was logging in yet more information, he felt something he hadn't felt for too long. It was a tear. He brushed it away but noticed that more kept coming. He was crying. Why was he crying? For a moment he had to take stock; the information he was receiving was not about a worse evil, but its opposite. He had discovered goodness.

The details were significant. A community had acted together to save the lives of over two thousand Jewish children evacuated from Paris by giving them shelter in their poor, rugged Pyrenees village. Through the course of the war, the children were housed, fed, protected, and schooled as if family, right under the noses of the German Gestapo. Such complicity, if discovered, brought certain death. Yet more train loads arrived, and more children were given sanctuary.

Years after the war was over, he was again deeply moved when he learned from survivors, who had returned to France to give thanks and to discover the secret to such heroism, that they instead had found only a people still going about their business as usual, business that was steeped in the rituals of mutual support, trust and responsibility. We only did what we always did, they claimed. Their acts of concerted devotion had grown not from a sudden or unfamiliar demand for action, but from the entrenched habits of their communal life. "Habits of goodness," our speaker declared.

Is there a parallel story here, one that identifies our role as teachers? I think so. As I sit listening to teachers talk about their efforts to help children act with assertive interest, with empathy, with respect and kindness, I hear the echoes of that story. It strikes me that many teachers seek to teach "habits of goodness." When we establish a social curriculum, when we struggle to integrate ethical practice into our daily fare, we too are trying to set down habits that we want children to carry from their desks to the pencil sharpener, out into the halls, the playground and even into the world. And we dare to envision that world far more filled with civility and honesty, with community and nonviolence than it is now. Our vision starts with our own classrooms and our own schools.

It is the task of creating habits of goodness that I believe infuses and inspires the work of each of the case studies in this volume. It is a task that inspires the work of many teachers. We teach habits of goodness most often in the way we organize the social and academic lives of our students and in the way that we bring the children into the regular activities and ceremony of the day. Thus, the children become a part of our rituals, and as we infuse those rituals with active, lively meaning, meaning that is constructed in collaboration with the children, our rituals become real for them. They help them know and practice a way of being. They help them construct a way of thinking. Faced with new situations, faced with difficult choices, faced with uncertainty, they turn to the knowledge they have gained from these rituals for support and guidance.

We often think of habits as small, trivial constructions—thoughtless, if well-intentioned, gestures learned by rote from nagging mothers and drill cards: reciting the times tables, brushing teeth, hanging up a shirt, making the bed. "Bad habits" tend to assume disproportionate importance. Think of how much money, time, and will-power goes into undoing bad habits: breaking the drug habit, the eating habit, the drinking habit, the smoking habit. It seems well evidenced that our bad habits meet elementary cravings, unspoken but irrepressible needs. Is it also possible that habits of goodness meet equally fundamental needs? Do we underestimate and therefore miss the power of good habits? Do we even really believe that actions taken for the good can be generated by habits that have become deeply entrenched? What does it take to form a good habit and what is implied when we transform the negative connotation of "habit formation" to a positive sense?

The other day I received a call from a high school senior who was applying to intern in the school where I teach. She had learned about the school from her local lacrosse teammates who had attended my school. "They were so friendly, so quick to give compliments," she explained. "In my high school, everyone was so tense, competitive, insulting. I figured these kids must have experienced something really different!" Were these Greenfield Center School students different or had they simply formed different habits, different ways of acting? They, in fact, had been exposed repeatedly to the act of paying compliments. From the time they were five, they had experienced weekly "representing meetings" where they learned to share their work and notice what others did. They had taken part in "authors' circles" where they were expected to listen and offer constructive feedback. They had been part of many discussions after soccer games when even the most insecure players were given sincere compliments for a good play. These rituals were repeated in class after class, year after year to give voice and also inclination to behavior that then transferred out onto the playing field, where no teacher watched.

In my work as a teacher I have struggled to name, to recognize, and to value the more simple classroom tasks I do. I have come to understand how much I learn through watching, trying out, doing, through developing a practiced eye to note actions well-meant or not, a ritual recalled or forgotten, a faked smile, a real handshake; and I know now how much learning is possible when we integrate social and ethical practices into the children's day to day school activities.

I am aware that as I advocate for adding an ethical component to our teaching I risk the danger that teachers may confuse teaching children habits of goodness with indoctrinating them with particular ideas. Indoctrination arises, I think, from the faulty premise that ethical beliefs are implanted, rather than constructed. It is our purpose in the formation of a social curriculum to help children construct ethical understanding through the careful, artful filter of experience. Experience in school comes from a composite of what I call the "instructional" and "situational" components of learning. It comes from a gooey blend of using both direct, facilitated teaching and unexpected opportunities that arise for us to apply the teaching. In this way we provide children with an experiential grounding that teaches them both to act and to think, to question and to reflect. "Why do we have to have assigned partners?" "Why do we have to sing if we don't feel like it?" "I don't want someone to invite me to their party if I'm not really wanted." "What if you don't really want *everyone* to come?" There is danger in not listening, not responding to the real questions and problems. We must neither pretend there is a known answer for complex ethical dilemmas nor assume that providing answers is somehow preferable to showing a willingness to think, to reason, to question and to search.

Indoctrination is certainly *not* what I am advocating. When we see that children are following the rules largely compelled by a compulsion to fit in, to achieve specified status or to gain some rewards, we have reason to question our teaching methods and our beliefs. I sometimes find it necessary to engineer—even demand—compliance at those moments when children seem to lack the capacity for exercising good judgment. Sometimes children cannot let go of cruel impulses or self-destructive patterns. At these times we need to redirect and manage if we are to hold up constructive aims. But we must not only direct and manage.

We need to act with meaning and conviction. Meaning continues to be the greatest motivator of all. Children crave meaning. Some children may not yet be able to invent the meanings they crave, the meanings that give order and safety. But when adults provide meaning, children can reach, stretch and exert themselves beyond their impulses. They can engage in figuring out issues of fairness, of safety, of inclusion, of harmony, of justice. They can find space at the table for "an outsider," pass the ball to an unequal player, give a compliment that counts, make a piece of work beautiful. For this they need guidance from adults.

I recently heard of a situation where a class was making a feast. A few children had forgotten to bring in the assigned ingredients. This class was attempting to generate the rules and the consequences as a way to be more responsible and accountable. Thus a "consequence" was chosen by the students and permitted by the adults, with the intention of being fair. The consequence called for the "forgetters" to watch but not participate in the feasting. Did these children perceive the difference between being mean-spirited and being just? Here was an opportunity for adults to raise the level of conversation to include elements of compassion, respect and empathy. The opportunities for children to participate in important decisions that affect their classroom must be coupled with adult guidance and guidelines if they are to learn truly ethical behavior, not just the exertion of power. Our best rituals offer ethical structures as well as meaningful student involvement.

I remember another episode in which the teacher invoked a problem solving ritual but also helped the children "chew on" the thorny issues so that "right" and "kind" were both considered. Gerald wanted to use Gretchen's new markers. Everyone at the table was using them. Gretchen refused. "You always break things," she said with conviction (and with reason). Gerald was crushed. The teacher, however, was not, because this was a teachable moment. The children had the challenge of a difficult issue where a perfect solution did not exist. But the teacher helped the class search out one which dignified Gretchen's wish to preserve her markers and which also dignified Gerald's need for acceptance, for inclusion in this activity.

I have seen children work these kinds of problems out in a way that strives for fairness and acknowledges the validity of the competing points. I recall that Gretchen set up her terms; it was understood that anyone could use her markers if they were willing to abide by her terms. That included Gerald. And I recall that Gerald used those markers with the utmost vigilance and care, watchful of each top, gentle as he could be to preserve the points. Again, the teacher constructed this outcome with her children. She set up ground rules: she noted Gerald's hurt and Gretchen's desire both to share and also to keep her markers nice. The class wrestled with ways to be honest and fair. The capacity to wrestle, to look for ways to act in the world that let us take better care of ourselves, each other and our things, is what I take to be goodness. Those day-to-day rituals, actions, conversations, and solutions that help us observe routine behaviors with a critical and wondering eye, and those times when as teachers we look squarely at the confusions, the conflicts, the strains, and the errors, those times when we encourage small steps, notice a step in the right direction, applaud new usage, celebrate a hard but successful struggle, that is what we take on in the task of teaching habits of goodness. It is then in the rhythm of ritual and real, in setting up ways to practice, in encouraging the risks of learning and invoking a real spirit of problem-solving that we inspire what Nel Noddings called "the quest for the moral journey." (Noddings, 1984)

In the first example the teachers abdicated their control to the detriment of the children. In the second example the teacher helped engineer an outcome to promote the children's growth rather than just to keep the classroom under control. Teachers are in a position of power. That power is vested in us by the nature of our work and we must use that power judiciously. At fifty, I can still remember the names of all my elementary school teachers, even my kindergarten teacher. I even remember which ones liked me. At times, I can recall flashes of shame when I displeased or failed to produce. I also remember those sacred moments when I earned praise.

Teachers are also in a position of authority. When we say listen, most often children will listen. When I tell a child to stop some silliness or to come with me, my voice firm and ringing with intention, most of the time that student obeys me. I also know that what we condone and condemn teaches a way of valuing—in words, in our actions and in our silence. When we walk by a mess in the hall, even if it isn't our doing, and pick it up, we say something. When we choose to stop a math lesson because kids are insulting each other, we say something. When we share a sorrow or a joy in our personal lives, we express connection, the worth of knowing, the trust of sharing.

We know that those children we single out for bad behavior, for breaking the rules, particularly the chronic ones, need our empathy or they are in danger of being known as "bad kids." I have walked into classrooms where I am a complete stranger and have had a fourth grader point out a peer and say, "He's real bad." Good and bad easily follow our "gold star" charts, our discipline procedures and our implicit attentions.

The power vested in authority is always a fragile creation. Teachers must know that they can create a safe environment. We must be able to encourage and urge learning even for those reluctant and shy souls, not to mention the feisty, smart-aleck ones who test and protest before the assignment is even on the board! Control is an essential quality of any capable teacher. And it is an awesome responsibility. Invariably, nights before school begins, I have dreams in which I am asking children to form a circle and they go helter-skelter. The fear of losing control, when so much rests on assuming control, runs deep in the teaching psyche. Teaching makes us so vulnerable in that fluid drama of new people to know, new and unpredictable events to encounter.

When I ring the bell for silence, I need to know there will be silence. Often I need silence because I know that the working tone of the room is essential. Perhaps directions must be given. Perhaps there is a change of plans. Perhaps there is a fire. Perhaps I have a headache. If I ring the bell, our signal for silence, and no one stops, I have no simple way to achieve order, to communicate, to ensure the well-being of the group. Control, always an essential attribute of teaching, must be used to promote the growth of the child, the learning, the classroom. It must not be used to make the teacher a bigger boss. The external control that I deem so vital is paradoxically in the service of self-control. What good is all my ability to control others, if it never translates into self-control, if the behavior, the ability to even stop and listen, has no relevance to what happens on the playground, in the street, or in the bedroom? The charge to achieve control as a teacher is also the charge to instill self-control, to build a willingness and a temper for self-governance. A teacher in control creates the rightful steps that coax out independence and exploration; she shows the children wonderful ways to use the blocks to build sturdy buildings and then gives them room to build. She encourages her class to figure out a way to decide on game captains, but helps them set up realistic criteria for "good leadership." Self-awareness and humility are the guard rails for teachers. Geoffrey Canada warns us that "When children feel that adults cannot or will not protect them, they devise ways of protecting themselves." He also notes that "In schools that allow children to get out of control, this has a ripple effect on other children. They start posturing, they become more violent, they become less manageable." (Canada, 1995, p. 25)

When we talk about "goodness," I want to make clear that it is *not* a label that some will achieve and others will not, that some have and others lack. We all have our better and worse selves, as my friend and colleague Roxann Kriete says. We all have times and places where we need to expose and vent that worse self in order to get to the better self. That is what I take to be the human condition, our shared humanity. Accepting goodness as a teachable and desirable attribute is really accepting a struggle and acknowledging a need. As we talked about this book, Roxann noted how "incredibly heartening and hopeful" it was "to begin to ally the words habit and goodness."

When I think about habits of goodness, I do not think about a life without conflict, without testing, without mistakes and problems, but I do think about a collaboration that brings together children, teachers, parents, and custodians as stakeholders in a common cause. The cause is to envision goodness—a goodness founded on mutual respect, on assertions of kindness and responsibility for the real work that needs to be done.

THE CASE STUDY PROCESS AND

THE SOCIAL CURRICULUM

CHAPTER ONE
DIGNIFYING THE STRUGGLE
Teachers as Problem Solvers

> "Power is the ability to take one's place in whatever discourse is essential
> to action and the right to have one's part matter."
> —Carolyn Heilbrun, *Writing A Woman's Life*

A common misconception is that good teachers do *not* have problems. Even experienced teachers make mistakes and handle things badly. The issue is not how to make teaching problem-free, but how to dignify and honor the problem-solving process that is inherent to good teaching. We must pay attention to the questions, the evidence, and the sources that yield our best results and find the time to share with our colleagues the realities of our classroom so we can solve problems together. It is often hard to stomach the missteps and often harder to recognize the successes. Teaching can be a lonely business. We need time to reflect when we are still alert and not on call, but reflection is so rare and so sacred. Yet it does happen and did happen with these case studies.

CHOOSING THE TEACHERS

This book features six case studies, each concerning a social curriculum problem. These case studies come from the real life of classrooms, although names and many identifying characteristics of students and situations were changed in order to respect privacy.

Six experienced teachers took part. They came from rural public schools and inner city schools, from the early primary grades and the upper grades. They selected classroom problems that truly interested them—new problems that had no simple or pat answers. As experienced professionals, they were asked to share their questions and frustrations and they were asked to share their learning.

So many of the teachers I have been fortunate to observe over the years, teachers in Washington, DC and West Haven, in inner city schools and rural ones, have been the experienced professionals—the high implementers of change in their schools and the veteran teachers. I continually meet teachers who, even after twenty-five plus years, are still attending workshops, reading new texts, and starting each new year with new concepts and a new room arrangement. Indeed, I recall my sheepish suggestion, on a hot, stuffy DC August day, that we move the clothes wardrobe in Ms. Harris' third grade room. We were busy doing room arrangement. This would be an ideal space, I said, for a library corner. (We were moving the desks from rows to create areas to allow choice and group work.) It turned out that the wardrobe was bolted down and nailed into the wall. After a few tugs, I gave up but Pat Harris certainly did not. She pulled from her desk a screwdriver which she jiggled until the wall released this monstrosity. Then, Ms. Freeman went to get the custodian who came muttering various oaths. It was a sight to see—all of us sweating and cheering on the custodian as the bulky wardrobe made its way across the room to its new location. As Ms. Freeman and Ms. Harris urged on a new room design, a new program, they kept saying aloud to the custodian, "Now, now, Mr. M., it's for the good of the children!" These were the kind of teachers I approached—talented teachers who were still, after many years on the job, pushing themselves, not just the furniture, to make changes for the good of the children.

CHOOSING THE PROBLEMS

For problems, the teachers did not focus on the class disruptions or children who disrupted, but rather the more systemic roadblocks that inhibited growth—problems that required new arrangements, different methods, a changing perspective. All six teachers focused their attention on problems related to the social curriculum. They all chose problems that grew from and centered around teaching social and ethical skills. The social curriculum is now considered, along with the academic curriculum, central to many school programs. Although teachers have always inserted lessons on civility and citizenship, taking turns and showing compassion, the need for more consistent and coherent instruction is readily apparent. A well developed social curriculum promotes academic growth. Classrooms which have social comfort and respectful discipline allow teachers to teach and children to learn. Through the creation of a solid social curriculum, the skills, attitudes, and work habits that we value evolve and flourish. We are teaching our

PETER WRENN

five year olds and fifteen year olds to say good morning, to listen to each other, to follow through on their jobs, to talk through their anger, to ask for help. Today's teachers, I believe, confront a mammoth task— to teach all children and not just those who seem ready to learn. We are engaged in the struggle to organize our schools to live (not just profess) the democratic ideals of opportunity and justice for all. We know we have our work cut out for us. We know we have problems.

Why Choose Case Studies?

The knowledge of how teachers think about and work to resolve classroom problems, knowledge that is so often private and a process that often takes place in isolation, needs to be made more accessible, more public. The facet of teaching that makes it a risky business, that leaves even experienced teachers often so vulnerable, needs to be shared. At any moment, things can and do go wrong.

In the isolation of our rooms, we are sometimes subject to the unpredictable failure of a lesson plan, a child's sudden eruption, a parent's disapproval, a judgment of a stranger who peers in for that very moment when everything is a jumble, and the worst critic, ourselves.

So many teachers I know fall asleep counting students (not sheep), reckoning with dismay the one or two or three children that were missed that day. Was she in school? Did I talk to her? Unfinished business. Teaching is risky business. Teaching involves risk-taking. To ask teachers to reveal a problem that may or may not be resolved, to investigate the resistance as well as the progress, is to ask a lot.

For the six teachers engaged in this project and for the readers and editors, the case studies project offered time to share, to ask questions, to work together. Even as the year wound down and everything turned hectic, the conversations continued.

Years ago when I began working with children in science, I found that the first step was to get them to look, really look. We were studying crickets as a fall unit in third grade. All the students had their own containers with numbers of these live creatures. They were to observe for thirty minutes and record everything they noticed. Frankie wrote a page that easily could have been straight from the encyclopedia. He knew it all. He had observed nothing. It took weeks to separate Frankie from his answers, to get him to pose even one curious question. He finally got hooked on whether the crickets had ears and that initiated his learning. His armory of facts seemed to distance him from the live creature, the very thing he most needed and was afraid to encounter. It was through Frankie and my struggle to help him that I began to understand the way I too use answers to distance myself from uncertainty and curiosity. Certainty is often needed to be a teacher and letting go of that can be difficult. I wanted a structure for these case studies that would free teachers to look at their classrooms from a new perspective and help them investigate something they really didn't understand.

If we were to capture the problem-solving process of teachers, we needed a format that would fit an ongoing classroom. I saw the structure as a storytelling. When we retell our days, when we grapple with thorny incidents, we often do so in the shape of a story. A case study seemed like an effective way to tell the story.

In these stories teachers are the narrators as well as main characters. The plot revolves around tensions, conflicts, convolutions in the narrative. As a main character, and as a biased narrator, the teacher's voice is central. It is central to observation, reactions, and tone. The teacher brings a perspective, a point of view, knowledge and decisive action. The children (and other teachers) are also characters in the story. Even when cast as the antagonist, the narrator knows better and struggles to ally with the children, to promote learning. The "fiery dragons" of our story may well be the social ills we encounter, the burdensome administrative policies, the entrenched and hard-to-move customs, hurts or prejudices. The battles we take on, in order to win, or just to get to the other side of "our problems" become the catharsis on the way to resolution. Some endings are happier than others. Some will just hang, waiting for next year. All, I believe, leave us wiser.

CASE STUDY PROCEDURES

Problem Statements

The procedure for these case studies started with a standard outline and common procedural steps. Each teacher began by describing a concern or aggravating issue in a *problem statement*. Sometimes the issue was reflected in a simple incident. In Linda Mathews' first grade class there was a glitter spill that somehow needed more intervention than seemed reasonable. This triggered questions for Linda about how her children were solving conflicts and why they continually needed her help even with the small glittery messes. Linda has been teaching for a long time and runs a very organized and fluid first grade room. Her students move briskly into choice areas. They are industrious and happy. So she wondered why she was so bothered by the glitter. In all the problem statements, an underlying matter of importance emerged. For Linda Mathews, the issue of self-reliance was central. It grew out of her own life experiences and her strong goals for children.

Eileen Mariani was unsettled by the rote responses of her kindergarten children in Morning Meeting. Arona McNeill-Vann was provoked by a newspaper article that questioned certain conflict resolution methods as good developmental practice for inner city children. Colette Kaplan was irritated by the plaints of "It's boring" from her fifth graders. Dottie McCaffrey thought that there ought to be more choice in her sixth grade room. And Cathy Jacques had just intercepted another hallway antic. She wondered, "Why don't the controls transfer?"

Reflections

The problem statement which focused on the classroom was followed
by teacher reflections. Why does this problem matter to me? What do I
want really? Why do I want it? Each teacher used a process of goal setting that I call establishing the "clear positives." Clear positives are statements which identify a desirable goal and expectation in specific language. The teacher shares them with the class. They become a rallying
cry for teacher and class, a way to share in the problem-solving efforts.

Observations

Teachers made observations after their first problem statement and as
a part of their ongoing assessment. The first observation provided important details for understanding the precise issue. Cathy began to observe the frequency of "play fighting" as a common social interaction.
Linda noted that not all problems were treated the same by her children. Colette noticed that "boring" occurred when some kids were
stuck, finished or not involved. Dottie discovered her students' lack of
communication skills. Eileen observed a critical moment of learning.
Observations were key. Teachers recorded data and used that data to
understand their problem.

Interventions

Interventions grew from the clear positives. Interventions included discussing problems with children, naming the problems, determining actions, altering and modifying approaches. They also included encouraging students in different ways and finding new ways to measure
progress. It seems important to note that both language and action
were critical to all the strategies and both evolved in conjunction with
each other.

Collegial Conferences

Each teacher identified another teacher or administrator in the same
school district with whom she could discuss her case study. Being able
to share with someone who knew the children or who could observe
the class helped teachers find new ways to think about their problems
and different strategies for dealing with them. Another level of communication came out of the work with editors. Letters and phone calls

produced questions, suggestions, and wonderful conversations. Finally, all the case study teachers and editors gathered together to read, share and discuss. It was a time of rich reflection, tireless discussion and critical learning.

Conclusions

Conclusions were a necessary last step. They were intended to center on outcomes and evaluation, to document progress and assess problem-solving approaches. They were also intended to offer a perspective on the process and its impact. If you read Colette's case study to learn, for example, how to get your fifth graders never ever to say the word "boring" again, you may be slightly disappointed. I'm not sure Colette found the definitive cure. She did, however, discover wonderful insights into a fascinating issue—one which ended up truly engaging her students in higher learning. Each case developed its own rich, complex and snarly tentacles. Each meandered and yet gathered force. Each offered critical insights into the problematic activity of the classroom. And so very importantly, each helps us know a bit more about the profound capacity of teachers to dignify the struggle to solve problems. These emerge, for me and I hope for you, as true invitations to learn.

CHAPTER TWO

SOCIAL CURRICULUM
Shared Assumptions

> "We need to approach the issues of classroom management and discipline as much more than what to do when children break rules and misbehave. Rather than simply reacting to problems, we need to establish an ongoing curriculum in self-control, social participation and human development."
>
> —Ruth Charney, *Teaching Children to Care*

The social curriculum is defined by its integration in an overall curriculum. It addresses how we conduct ourselves at all times. It cannot be confined to a period a week devoted to respect. It influences the room organization, the daily schedule, the rules, the expectations for individual and collaborative work, the work outside the classroom walls, and the measures of progress and achievement. It encourages, enhances and enriches the academic curriculum; it never replaces it. The social curriculum has its best chance of success when it becomes part of a school culture, part of the concerted effort that spans years and years of schooling, and when it provides opportunities to test and learn, mindful of developmental conditions necessary for growth. It will not work as an add-on, or a study unit or a monthly feature. The reality of a social curriculum is that it requires persistent conviction and our best teaching resources.

The academic curriculum and social curriculum must be interconnected. Educator Chip Wood asks, "What good is intelligence if it is used for evil purposes?" The social curriculum is our way of saying that learning needs to promote goodness in this world. It is of little use if it is used to promote destructive ends. We want to nurture intelligent, competent, industrious and skillful beings. We also want them to use their brains not to design lethal weapons but to invent more energy-efficient cars, to find ways to feed the hungry, to add to the creative resources of the world. One of the most pressing questions demanded by children is "What is the point of schooling?" Why should they learn to read or write? Does anyone really care? We see children struggling with alienation and negativity. We see them question the value of school not only as it relates to their chances in an unpredictable job market, but also as it relates to their personal growth. We see children overcome by stress so that every grade feels like a final judgment, an agent of terror. The quest for a purpose to school does not lie in any competition between our social and academic objectives. It is only going to emerge through the convergence of these claims.

What exactly is the relationship between classroom management and a social curriculum?

The social curriculum is *not* classroom management. I use the concept of classroom management to refer to the ways we establish expectations for behavior, the ways we generate and implement rules, the consequences we enforce when rules are not followed. Management refers to how we teach our expectations. We try to influence both how children act and how they think. Classroom management sets up structures which make productive relationships and interactions possible between students and teachers and between classmates. I have discovered from personal experience that an orderly, safe and engaging classroom is central to learning and school life. Discipline and management provide a positive learning and constructive force, one that affirms the potential of schooling.

My understanding of management has grown out of mistakes and poor preparation. Without a way to manage, I cannot teach. Our best lesson plans hinge on our ability to establish discipline—whether the paint goes on the easel or on the floor, whether the books are thrown or read, whether the pasta is sorted or catapulted, whether the room is industrious or rank with tension—and whether we teachers and students care enough or know enough to make discipline count.

Why we manage and what we hope to achieve through a system of management are what I mean by a "social curriculum." The social curriculum refers to our intentional efforts to develop the social and ethical capacities of each individual and to build a respectful, inclusive and safe community life. We want our system of classroom management to achieve the aims of our social curriculum. It is critical to examine the decisions of how we manage under the scrupulous gaze of these aims. We need to see whether the strategies we use are compatible with our social aims. When we line up the boys on one side and the girls on the other, are we helping children to work together or stay firmly inside gender roles? When we reward right answers and pass over (or scold) wrong ones, are we encouraging divergent thinking or reinforcing right-answer thinking? When we make all the choices and impose unquestioned rules, do we give opportunity to learn self-control or make decisions? When our rules are broken, do we accomplish our goals more effectively by doling out punishment or by working on problem-solving that will foster student responsibility? I am continually aware that even the most mundane and incidental practice has implications beyond that incident.

The aims of the social curriculum need to be translated into both limits (what is not acceptable) and guidelines (what we want to achieve). I offer here an example of an incident in which it was so clear that both setting limits and encouraging constructive behaviors were important to achieve a positive social change. A few years ago, one of the older students deliberately broke every window on one side of his classroom building. We approached his behavior and the issues it raised from two angles. The first was that he had behaved unacceptably and there

CHERRY WYMAN

would be consequences for that behavior. We asked him to stay after school for two weeks to help the custodian repair the windows. (This part involved adult supervision and time. He was not very competent at first and took a while to learn to wield the glazing compound effectively!) The second angle we took involved acknowledging his discontent with school. We talked to him and made it clear that we wanted to help make school a place he could feel better about. This led to some constructive problem-solving during which we brainstormed together some ideas that might make school more tolerable to him. We came up with an office job at which he worked each day for half an hour. It gave him a time away from the group, a time to assert independence, a time to practice self-control, and a time to feel important in ways that his academic struggles often didn't provide.

Several goals from the social curriculum guided us in this incident. We wanted this boy to treat his environment with care, to be able to communicate his frustrations and anger with adults who could help find a positive solution rather than vent these feelings in acts of petty vandalism. We wanted him to walk through the tasks of his day with self-respect and self-control. To help him grow toward these goals, we used a number of classroom management techniques: we imposed logical consequences for his misbehavior, allowing him to make reparation and assume responsibility. We held a conference with him which helped him (and us) identify some of the reasons for his acting out. We shared our hope and conviction that school could become an acceptable place to him, and demonstrated our willingness to shape his program in ways that would honor his input. Together we agreed upon expectations that he felt he could meet with these conditions in place.

We must be realistic. He did not turn into a model student. But neither did he damage school property again. He did make progress in his attitude towards the school and himself. And he is now doing well in high school.

FOUR COMMON ASSUMPTIONS

Four common assumptions define a social curriculum as understood and practiced by the teachers of these case studies. They are not intended to be inclusive or fixed but provide an introduction to the thinking that guided our conversations and case study work.

Assumption One: Education helps children develop self-control and a sense of community.

John Dewey stated that "The ultimate aim of education is to create the power of self-control." (Dewey, 1938) I think of self-control as the power to attend, to wait your turn, to be patient, to amuse yourself if need be. It means being able to approach conflicts without first resorting to fists and abusive name-calling; it means acting with purpose, with direction and decision. Finally, it means being able to act in a way that shows respect for rules and traditions and accepts the defined limits which are necessary to assure the rights of others. Without the ability to do these things, I do not believe that children can be contributing community members. Conversely, for children to feel that they can take care, they must feel taken care of. If the environment is not safe, we cannot expect the children to be in control. Building control and building community are interrelated aspects of a social curriculum.

Community offers a sense of place. If it is to be a place we wish to be, it will meet our needs for belonging, for significance and for fun. Community has the power to draw us together through shared ideals, common goals, and a wide repertoire of familiar songs, stories, games, folk wisdom. It has the potential to embrace differences of personality, of interest, of styles of learning. In a democratic vision of community, we work for consensus while welcoming diversity of opinion. School should be a place where we learn to balance responsibility and freedom, individual interests and collective needs, work and fun.

Dewey used the word "create." Self-control need not be inherent. Self-control and community can be taught systematically and patiently through experience in school. A social curriculum pays careful attention to children's social and ethical development through the medium and context of school life.

Assumption Two: A social curriculum uses two distinct but interrelated levels of teaching—Instructional and Situational.

A) INSTRUCTIONAL This concept describes our intentional practice, a practice that is often woven into ritual. We teach specific social skills and ethical thinking in ways that are deliberate and developmentally appropriate. It is here that we structure conversations, activities and opportunities to practice. We provide models. We role play. We rehearse

PETER WRENN

and give homework. Every morning, for example, in our Morning Meeting, we practice active listening, interested comments, good questions, attentive participation, safe fun. Every afternoon during clean-up time, we practice picking up papers, organizing shelves, caring for materials, interdependence and work habits. We know that a high degree of regularity, consistency and carry over is necessary for learning to take hold. Indeed, we worry about the student who does the math problems only so long as we sit nearby and orchestrate. We also look to develop a spirit and willingness to participate in the learning.

B) SITUATIONAL   By this I mean how the instruction transfers to regular school activity. Active listening needs to be carried over into reading groups; caring for materials needs to continue during work with projects; good questioning should occur during math lessons; and respectful interactions should occur at all times. Noticing, recognizing and working with children as they attempt to use what they learn in their day-to-day lives requires situational teaching. We know from learning theory that children often construct understanding through their own experience, that concepts are often developed through those encounters that create some disequilibrium and unease. In situational learning, teachers use the incidents on the playground, the cuts in line, the sloppy assignments as "teachable moments." They stop the reading group to remind and reinforce the need for real attention when peers share. The continual meshing of instruction with situation, what we will often call ritual with real, is critical to building a solid social curriculum practice.

Assumption Three: "It is dangerous to let children be seen or see themselves as bad."—Sara Ruddick, Maternal Thinking

As we attempt to work with those incidents and situations where children act badly, we must continuously remind ourselves that we are in no way sorting children into good and bad piles. Children, as we know, can act with cruelty and meanness. As teachers we certainly could offer a long recital of acts that include bullying, name-calling, deceit, vandalism, and shoddy effort. We intercept our share of stealing, mean note passing, and cheating. To say that children should not be "seen" as bad is not to ignore or not act on those times when they behave badly. Many children break rules, act with calculated cruelty, test limits. If we are to help them grow, it will be because of our ability to appeal to some potential for good, an expressed faith in their ability to choose differently, to learn another way.

   We do well to invoke the phrase, "Stress the deed, not the doer," (Charney, 1992, p. 161) and to notice and attend to the unwanted behaviors while claiming the wanted children. "I don't like it when you make faces—but I like you." "I don't like that teasing, but I like you." Even with careful phrasing two teachers may say exactly the same words and yet one will convey firm guidance and the other rejection. With children, even children who defy the limits and break our most cherished rules, we must retain an empathy for the rule-breaker and an authentic faith in their potential to do good if we are to help them grow. We must show them that the choice to cheat is side by side with the choice to do honest work and that we each have the potential for each choice. Time-out and other consequences work best when they provide options for logical and respectful reparations.

Assumption Four: Language is an essential teaching tool. We must learn what Faber and Mazlish describe as "how to talk so kids will listen and listen so kids will talk." (Faber and Mazlish, 1982)

Language guides action. Surgeons need steady hands; teachers need steady language. We need a voice that is at times firm, at other times

gentle, at times reasoned, at other times playful, at times telling, asking, engaging, and directing. We must be able to structure conversations, to communicate effectively, to know when and how to use open-
ended questions that invite wondering and directive questions that
urge focus. We need to take time, as teachers, to develop a repertoire
of voices if we are going to meet the many demands.

We are used to presentation methods, questions which elicit a right
answer, stimulating lessons which narrate information. Now, in addition to traditional techniques, I am learning what Bob Strachota calls
the art of asking "real questions," questions which "allow the teacher
and students to wonder together." Bob believes in inviting children "to
tell me their thoughts and then try to follow their thinking so that I can
help them think further. This is a leap from telling, but a very satisfying leap." (Strachota, 1996, p. 45) The teacher's role is to identify the
real questions, to structure conversations that encourage honest thinking and a shared endeavor; it is not necessarily to provide answers.

Teachers are so often expected to know answers. When I consult,
I often feel so much pressure to have the answers that my first impulse
is to make them up rather than say "I don't know." With children and
with colleagues this may mean missing the most interesting conversations. There are certainly times when we do know the answer, when it
is foolish not to supply what is needed. To turn everything into an exploration would be absurd. Yet to generate and find meanings together, to build a common language, to embrace a struggle through
the skill of wordsmithing makes for very "pleasant collaboration." We
see this often in the case studies. Colette Kaplan's fifth graders set out
to "unbore themselves." Linda Mathews' first graders decide there are
"little and big conflicts." Arona McNeill-Vann's six year olds develop
rules for sharing a book.

An Illustration

I would like to offer an anecdote, a case study, as my example from one
of my classroom experiences which I hope will illustrate our shared
assumptions in the social curriculum. The story is intended to demonstrate the ways that aims and practice may converge.

It was April. I had just been on a short field trip with my seventh
and eighth graders. We had gone to see a wonderful Alvin Ailey dance

performance provided by the Fine Arts Center at the University of Massachusetts. The children were an enthusiastic audience. As we waited for our bus to arrive, I noticed something that I didn't like. The class of forty students had knotted into tight bands of cliques. We had worked on this at the onset of the year and there they were again. A group of the "in set" was making lots of noise, laughing too loudly, making secretive gestures, casting eyes to see if anyone was really watching, trying to get more than their due attention. I could see that there were smaller clutches of friendships that wandered away indifferent to the rest. But I also saw that longing, watchful stance that froze others into a periphery—watching, wishing to be included, unable to relax or ignore. It didn't feel comfortable. It felt tense.

What to do about it? Initially, I went through excuses. It was impossible for adolescents to survive without cliques—so why bother? Then I asked myself what had I done wrong and why hadn't I seen it coming? Where had I been? Mostly, I had been busy with my classes, reading papers, trying to pull together the final term's instructional work. And, of course, it was spring—spring with its extra flurry of adolescent social energies, finding ways to explore and test out the turf of romance, of flirtation, of attraction, of personal status. Even with a distance that I am grateful comes with age, even knowing that these roles and places shift repeatedly as one grows up, I felt that sadness that exclusion recalls. It did not seem right to let it pass, to view it with a philosophical detachment, to ignore it. I clung to our "critical contract," the goals we had created for ourselves as a class. Wasn't one to be more inclusive?

The next day we (the other teachers and I) called the group together for an "honest discussion"—our term for class meetings. I shared what I had seen the day before, starting with the positives: they were such an attentive audience; they took wonderful care with the younger children; they waited with patience and control; they enjoyed the event. But I also told them that I noticed the cliques and that they bothered me. What did they notice? In the moments of silence, before hands were raised and before I called on anyone, I surveyed the group. Something akin to relief was spreading. (So often when a problem is named, there is this sense of relief, I realize.) There was a stillness. There was a hunched forward look. The twiddling and fiddling had ceased. Everyone waited. It was on their minds, too. Their observations flowed readily and largely acknowledged that the room had indeed become very cliquey. Too cliquey. A few dissenting voices spoke, but strikingly, even those who seemed most assured and confident of a central spot recognized the cliques and that we had a problem.

Why, I asked, is it a problem if you are in the clique? One of the students spoke up, articulating things that registered so profoundly, recalling so well the stress of not just my younger days, but the reality of group life. "When you are like in the main clique, you're always afraid that something will happen and you won't be part of it. That you'll miss something . . . so you're afraid to be by yourself, or to be doing something different, even if you want to."

I am best prepared for these discussions if I can remember two things. One is that children do not break rules because they are "bad." Rather most rules are broken to try out a more willful self, to gratify impulse or to test the limits. And for a few, as someone recently said of a youth who took potshots with his BB gun into a crowd, it is because "there is so much pain mixed inside." Second, my role is not to promote one side's claims against another, not the "in" set against the "out" set, but to help them consider their demands in terms of a larger,

PETER WRENN

better outcome. In this case the better outcome was the potential for a classroom where everyone felt welcome and accepted. Would that be more tempting than one in which a few would succeed and others would not? Children, I find, are not afraid to be idealistic.

Our classroom had become a place of cliques. But teachers couldn't fix the problem of exclusion; the children had to want to work on it. It was a serious challenge that would take honest effort, whatever that effort turned out to be. They would have to think hard and truthfully about whether they wanted to do that work. We sent them off to think and write in their journals. Question: Do you want to work on being less cliquey? Do you want to try to be more inclusive as a class?

Thirty-six out of 42 students said they wanted to be less cliquey. They wanted to work on the problem. A few said it didn't matter to them. One boy said he liked things the way they were. (He was for the first time "in.") They wanted to "un-clique."

This anecdote drew on all four assumptions.

Assumption One: Education helps children develop self-control and a sense of community.

The class behavior during our trip provided an opportunity to talk about the harmful effects that exclusive behavior produced and to re-consider the ideal of a more inclusive community where everyone felt welcome and accepted.

Assumption Two: A social curriculum uses both instructional and situational teaching.

In this example, the situation provided both the context for intervention and also concrete behaviors and alternative approaches for us to discuss. It also allowed us to revisit our class goals which we had formulated at the start of the year. Using the well-established instructional structure of class meetings, we asked the students to engage in an honest dialogue on how cliques would promote our goal of an inclusive class.

Assumption Three: It is dangerous to allow children to see themselves or be seen as bad.

It was important to establish the terms of the discussion in such a way that we were not creating a discussion about good versus bad kids. The "in" were not villainous, the "out" virtuous. We were careful to frame the problem so that the class felt the sense they were working toward a common goal rather than passing a moral judgment.

Assumption Four: Language is an essential teaching tool.

We phrased the problem carefully so we could engage students in a dialogue about the effects of cliques and we framed the problem as a real question—how can we work together to make our room more inclusive? We provided no recipes or mandates, just an ethical ideal and an expectation that students would work on a solution. Language helped us clarify our class goals and agree on action plans.

IN SUMMARY

The six case studies which follow are full of examples of thinking and teaching practices built upon the shared assumptions articulated in this chapter. Though the teachers involved bring many different experiences which shape their examination of the problems they have highlighted, these assumptions define the vantage point from which they look.

THE CASE STUDIES

PETER WRENN

PETER WRENN

CHAPTER THREE

RITUAL AND REAL

Developing Language in a Kindergarten Classroom

by Eileen Mariani

Eileen Mariani is a preschool/kindergarten teacher who lives and works in western Massachusetts. The mother of three adult sons, she is married to Paul Mariani, a teacher, poet and biographer. For several years she has worked as a consultant for Northeast Foundation for Children, giving workshops on *The Responsive Classroom*®² to teachers from Washington, DC to Maine. Her interests include reading, running, traveling and cooking.

THE SETTING

Mill towns all across New England are facing difficult times. There is always the threat of the paper mill closing and more families losing their jobs. For the past twenty-two years I have been the only kindergarten teacher in just such a town. About 160 children attend the local school with enrollments declining each year as families leave to find other work. Most children in the school are part of families with two adults, but not always their biological mothers or fathers. A large percentage of both adults work outside the home.

Fortunately, two major industries in town provide tax support and the school budget is well-funded. Support services such as counseling, special education, speech and language, and occupational therapy are plentiful. Classes in the school are small. The school has a preschool program that is voluntary, a kindergarten class and grades up through sixth. The twenty-three-year-old school is well-maintained and very attractive and families and staff take a great deal of pride in the school.

THE CHILDREN

Most of the children come from families that have been in town a long time and want to stay there despite the economic hardships. Ethnic influences seem to have filtered away as there are no first generation immigrant families. Families want their children to do well in school and feel it is the job of the teachers to see that they learn. For the most part, children bring to school a respect for teachers and an eagerness to be in school.

My kindergarten class this year is especially small. There are six boys and six girls who attend the half-day program. Most of the children have taken part in the preschool program and are familiar with the teachers and the routines. All the children are white and of similar backgrounds. There are four children who receive speech and language services but other than that there are no identifiable special needs. Most children in this class identify watching television as their favorite pastime. Their VCR libraries are well-stocked. In the fall during our before-school home visits, every family but one had the television on the entire time. All this information is background to what happens when the children arrive in class.

THE NIGHT BEFORE SCHOOL

You would think that after all these years of teaching, I would get over the anxiety of the first day of school. No, every September I have the same dream. The children are sitting in a circle on the floor waiting for me to say something. The preliminaries are over, the families are gone, the door is shut and we are alone—together. The children are silent as they stare at me with expressionless eyes. I open my mouth to speak and find I have nothing to say. I stare back, and after a few minutes, the children quietly leave the room—one by one. When I wake up I ask myself the same questions. Can I really do this again? Can I engage the children in conversation? Can I help them take pleasure in the discovery of learning?

The Problem

What in fact happened on the first day and the days that followed is that I did have much to say and the children did stay and listen. The real problem surfaced, however, when it was their turn to talk. It seems that over the years my students have become increasingly non-verbal and passive. This year, within the first few weeks, it became clear to me that the children in this group were no exception. They needed to be prodded to express themselves in a class discussion or to share something about themselves. When they did speak, they offered only the required amount of information.

Some Early Observations

This class became adept at the expected social language in a relatively short time. While observing them one morning in October, I noticed they would quickly say "good job" when someone showed their work, "I'm sorry" when someone was hurt, "please pass the milk" at snack time. When asked to share something about their weekend, they dutifully responded with a brief factual statement ("I ate at McDonald's." "I rode my bike."). I noticed at Choice Time that even when the children spent large amounts of time in one work area together, they rarely talked to one another except to ask for a material. Although I was happy to see that the children were generally treating each other respectfully, I ended my observation feeling saddened by the lack of genuine verbal interaction. I was especially saddened to see how easily children can get stuck in a ritual, responding only to the words and not to the intent of treating each other with respect. During this same Choice Time I happened to hear Megan shout at Sara, "You're being mean to me!" Megan had wanted some play dough and Sara had refused to give her any because she had failed to say "please." Megan was an impulsive child who was trying to be part of a group that tended to exclude her. She did not know how to correct her mistake and Sara was unwilling to help because she preferred not to include Megan in the play dough fun. I listened to their explanations for not sharing:

Sara: But she didn't say "please."

Teacher: So how should she ask for the play dough?

Jennifer: She should say, "Please can I have some play dough?"

Teacher: What if she forgets to say "please"?

Jennifer: Then she can't get any.

Teacher: What would a friend do to help?

Kate: I already gave her some. See?

Megan: And I said "thank you."

Teacher: But I see a different problem here. If a friend forgets the way to ask for something, how can you help?

Sara: She should say, "Please can I have some play dough?"

Teacher: What can we do now?

Kate: I don't know.

Jennifer: You can ask the right way.

Teacher: Let's practice it and see if we can help each other with this problem.

The problem was that they had learned to hide hurtful responses behind respectful talk. I needed to coach them through new ground.

Each year with each new class I have to figure out how to get the children to talk to me and to each other about what they are doing and

how they are feeling and what they are thinking. With this particular class, though, it felt like a much more difficult task because they were so few in number and so similar in their verbal responses. While it might seem very pleasant to "hold court" and just tell the children what to do and what to say, I know that is only the easy way out and that no real learning will occur.

So, I soon decided that this year I would focus on helping these children assert themselves using language to get them really talking. I wanted them to be able to talk with each other about what they were doing and learning and to talk about things that were important to them. And I wanted my classroom to be filled with talk that is meaningful, what I've come to call "real talk." I know it feels easier for the children to remain passive, to say nothing or to only say what the teacher requires. Yet, it is when my classroom is abuzz with "real talk" that I know that real learning is taking place.

SHARING TIME

Social interaction is very important to me. I want to be known and to know others. By nature I am an extrovert and I gladly choose the company of others over the solitude of the woods. Each weekend I run with a dear friend and sometimes we have to make a choice between running and talking—which way to use our breath. For some reason, the talking always wins and the waist line loses. My friend and I have solved all the problems of the world and then some. Since I am a people-person and feel very comfortable in social situations I would like my children to feel comfortable talking, too.

I decided to begin my quest for real talk during Morning Meeting, *sharing* which we have every day. Typically, we include a time during the meet- *in* ing for children to share their news. I thought I would use this time to *MM* help the children move beyond rote responses to real exchanges. My struggle took many different attempts. During the first two months of school we spent a lot of time learning the expected behavior during sharing times. By November, the children knew that they should speak loudly and clearly enough for their classmates to hear them and that the listeners should have their eyes on the speaker. Children listened without adding their own comments and the speaker tried to share in an interesting way. The routine was that I would present a focused question

more work

Come up with good open-ended questions for sharing and write on notecards

and we would go round robin as each child answered it. My hope was that this exercise would help the children get to know each other and that each child would feel known. Some of the questions I used this fall were: "What do you like about being a kid?" "What did you do over the weekend?" "What do you wish you could do when you are older?"

While the mechanics of the sharing time seemed to go well—the children were attentive to each other and mindful of our meeting rules—the substance of the interaction dissatisfied me. What follows is an example of one of these sharing times:

Teacher: What do you like about being a kid?
Joe: I like climbing trees.
Sara: I like to go to Riverside Park 'cause you get to go on the rides.
Danielle: I like to make different stuff and read.
Adam: To sleep over and to go to friends' places.
Amanda: I like playing in school, learning how to read and how to draw better.
Kate: I like playing house 'cause I have a little beauty center and it has a little tiny chair that my dad and mom can't fit in.
Jason: Disney World. I'm going there when I'm seven.
Cody: I like to build stuff with nails.
Mark: Put on plays.

Gradually the children were getting to know each other through sharing, but the process seemed to lack feeling or affect. So my next step was to ask a focused question based on a feeling. In December, I read Mercer Mayer's book *When I Get Mad* to the class. I then asked the children what makes them mad. Again we went around the circle and the answers went something like this: "I get mad when my sister messes up my room," "when I get dreams," "when my brothers are fighting with me and my friends," "when the power goes off and I can't watch my shows on TV," et cetera.

talk about feelings

TAKING A RISK

Even though they were sharing about a feeling, the children were still sharing in a rote way and there was no opportunity for them to comment on their classmates' remarks. What could I do, I wondered, to change the dynamics and make it more interactive and meaningful for the children?

When I brought this question to a colleague she suggested I use the "Questions and/or Comments" technique which I usually use during Representing Time. (This is a time each day when five children share with their peers something they have worked on that day and their peers offer questions and comments about the sharing.) The problem with this was that if each child asked for two questions or comments after their sharing, Morning Meeting would take too long. Even if I switched sharing to another part of the day, our program was only two and a half hours and the children would be spending too much time listening to each other.

Still, one day I decided to risk it just to be sure. I asked all the children to share about what they had done over the weekend and to ask for questions and comments. Mark began, "My dad got a new truck yesterday and we're going to bring it home today. Questions and comments?"

Ryan: What color is it?
Mark: Red and blue and green and pink.
Ryan: It must be cool. Did you ride in it yet?
Mark: Not yet. Jennifer.
Jennifer: What color is it inside?
Mark: Black and red.

for People have 2-3 questions/comments each day

All twelve shared and it lasted a very long forty-five minutes. In reflecting on what the children said I was impressed by how supportive they were of each other. I was convinced of the value of adding questions and comments for some of our sharing but still needed to work within the time constraints.

During the rest of the year I tried several more variations of Sharing Time. I started using a sign-up with only five children sharing a day. I also began theme-based Sharing Days during which children would bring in something from home around a specific topic such as collections from nature or something they had made or a favorite photo album.

An Insight

While I continued to struggle with making sharing meaningful, an incident occurred that gave me a new perspective on bringing real talk into the classroom. During a morning meeting in late winter Jennifer was reminded of our meeting rule about saving places for a friend. She moved her foot and then started to cry softly. I ignored her tears at first and waited for the rest of the class to take their places on their carpets. Jennifer continued to cry and the other children noticed and were concerned. I asked Jennifer if she would like to tell us what was bothering her or if she would like to go tell my teaching assistant privately. She chose to ignore me. I then began to acknowledge to the class that, "Yes, Jennifer is upset and that happens sometimes—we all get upset about different things." I shared that sometimes I get upset when I need to be somewhere and I am late.

At this point there was a chorus of children anxious to share about the times that they were upset. I began to call on the children who had their hands raised and their comments ranged from getting upset when the dog messes on the floor to being upset when their parents talk about divorce. I then asked the children what they could do if someone else were upset—like Jennifer. Joe suggested making a card for her. Kate suggested giving her your snack. Mark suggested being her friend. The discussion was lively and focused and meaningful to the children and to me.

In reflecting on this incident I knew that I had just reacted instinctively to Jennifer. I wanted to give her time to recover from her tears and still save face with her peers. I also felt that what was bothering her went deeper than a reminder about the rules. Yet she was in school now and she needed to participate in the day. The conversation that occurred, with all the children participating about things that upset them, took enough time so that at the end Jennifer shared too.

Here was exactly the kind of conversation I had wanted to encourage. From this incident I learned that when something happens that has real meaning to the children, I get "real talk." They were moving from their rote responses about contrived questions to genuine sharing about things that mattered to them. The routine had been shaken up and they and I were making connections between real events and real sharing. While I cannot plan for an incident like this one, I realize now that I need to take advantage of them when they do occur. There have been many times in my teaching when I have ignored the obvious question for one that I had written in my plan book.

A REAL DILEMMA BRINGS REAL TALK

Another case in point came in the spring. It had to do with a discussion that occurred after our class story at the end of the day. The children were getting ready to take the bus home. One child started to cry because Sara had promised him that she would sit next to him on the bus that day and he had just heard her promise the same thing to another child. He was feeling rejected and powerless. Before I could ask him about this, some other children chimed in with similar stories of Sara promising them the same thing on other days.

This was a real dilemma. What was I going to do? And what were the other children learning about Sara? Did I want them to view her as untrustworthy at five years of age? I tried to steer the discussion into more neutral territory. I asked, "What does it mean to make a promise to someone?" Most of the responses centered around the idea that you do what you say you are going to do. What finally evolved after quite a few minutes was the notion that a promise needed to be taken seriously, but since the bus was waiting to take the children home we agreed to continue the discussion the next day. The children decided that for this day Sara would sit with Adam because he was really upset. But the matter was not resolved.

After the children departed I was left with the problem of figuring out what direction I would take the next day. Were the children able to understand the meaning of the word "promise" and should they be held accountable to it at five years of age? And yet, where do we begin the process of teaching them that words have real meaning and emotions attached to them?

The next day I opened our discussion with this statement: "You know, I couldn't sleep last night because thoughts about our discussion about promises kept swirling around my head and I was wondering what you thought about our discussion." The children took the ball and ran with it. They were ready to solve the problem to their own sat-isfaction because they trusted the process. They knew how to listen and speak to each other in caring ways.

It was agreed that the word "promise" was to be used very care-fully and, as one little boy said, "only if you really mean to do some-thing because if you didn't the other people wouldn't believe you any-more." And as far as Sara was concerned, they agreed that she would take turns sitting with children who asked her but that she could de-cide whom she wanted to sit with, too—so one day it was her choice and the next day it was a child who asked. But if we were to keep our rule of being friendly to everyone in the class maybe they could take turns sitting with other friends.

The conversation lasted the better part of twenty minutes and dur-ing that time the children were completely engaged in meaningful con-versation. I was impressed by the attention they gave to this topic and the concern they showed for each other. The children were showing me that they could indeed take the ritual of sharing and apply it to sit-uations that had real meaning for them.

My Discoveries

Through looking at this issue of bringing real talk into my classroom, I found out many things about the children and about my teaching. I found out that children, even when they have limited language abili-ties and seem passive in many situations, can learn through practice and a caring environment to talk about things that are important to them and to engage in meaningful discussions.

I also learned that real talk will not occur just in the routines I have set up. It can be present there and these routines can help children learn to be skilled and comfortable users of language, but much of real talk grows out of real life. This year I learned a lot about using the daily problems and incidents of school life as starting points for en-gaging children in real conversation. And as I go about my rituals at the beginning of next year, I will be more patient with the process of making our talk real.

RUTH'S COMMENTARY *Ritual and Real*

"I want them to learn from the practice of these social skills (the greetings, the sharing, the choices) how to use them in real situations so that
they are internalized and ingrained in their character."

—Eileen Mariani

This case focuses on ways to help children move from ritualized responses to what Eileen calls "real talk." She feels frustrated when she
observes two of her children fight over who said "please" or "thank
you" for the play dough which they are both trying to hoard. Words
and meaning have become handily confused and she worries that the
children have become stuck in the very phrases and language that
should add to the well-being of the classroom. She wants her students
to talk to her and to each other. She wants them to figure out how to
share the play dough, rather than figure out who said thank you first
or last.

What seems evident from this case is that ritual behaviors and real
behaviors coexist in the classroom. The churning question for me becomes how we maximize and sustain an effective balance between
both those aspects of classroom activity. We need, as Eileen notes, to
make sure rituals do not sound like broken records. We need to be
there to help see that there is carryover and meaning. We need to provide opportunity for children to interact spontaneously while offering
instruction that will enrich their repertoire of social skills. If children
know each other's names, how to talk and listen, and how to express
feelings without charged insults, then they can confront unkept bus
promises or moments of upset.

Eileen, as a keen observer of her children, notices what they are
learning in the daily rituals of her classroom and when they are stuck
in the rituals. Yet she wants more for them. She wants to see them use
language in ways that expand their learning. Although the phase of
teaching the rituals is downplayed in this case study, it is important to
see that what has already happened is no small accomplishment.
Eileen observes the ways the children share in Morning Meetings, their
conversations (and lack of conversations) during their regular choice
times, and how they report on their work when it is time to share with
the class. She sees their comfort and understanding of their routines

grow; she sees them take what they have learned into child-initiated interactions. I observe a process of patient teaching that gives children access to habits of response and listening. Each morning as they sit in their circle and share what they like or think, however contrived, the expectation of response is developed. Speech is practiced. Sentences are formed. The children are developing the tools and resources that will later help them talk about promises and morning upsets and use real talk in real situations. Topics which seem contrived (which they sometimes are) may also be seen as times to practice. And what the children learn from their practice as the question moves from child to child around the circle is that even a simple telling is of value to the teacher and to the listening audience. Everyone has something worthwhile to say. Thus, everyone is expected to speak (not each day, but over time) and everyone is expected to listen. These are not simple skills. And if at first the questions seem a bit forced, a bit random, a bit contrived, at least they establish a safe participation. The questions cover easier topics of feelings, of work in school, and events at home. The structure is predictable and direct. The responses too sound predictable and routine. Yet they build steadily an expectation of speech, of response, of attention and interaction.

My own students generally are highly verbal coming from predominantly middle class backgrounds. They talk a lot—sometimes too much. Yet many of these children struggle to engage in meaningful conversations. Their "conversations" often allow little interaction. Initiation of conversation with someone other than a close friend is usually teacher-directed, not spontaneous. Sarcasm and low-level insults serve as humor. They have a desire to talk and a hunger to be noticed, but not the ability to sustain conversations and engage in meaningful talk without teacher facilitation. And without teacher input the quiet stay quiet, the loud stay loud and the subject flits and darts. I add these observations to suggest that the question of "ritual and real talk" is pertinent for all students, at all grades, across cultural and class lines, geography and race. Though they may manifest it differently, my students too struggle with "real talk."

Reporting about her students, Eileen told me, "When they are silent and obedient, I feel that they are acting as they may have been told to act in school, not as they more naturally would if they were involved in their own learning." Real talk, then, is a link to active learning, risk taking, question-asking and expression of understanding. Real talk "goes beyond rote social learning." Initially Eileen confided that she knew how to teach rituals, to get her students to say "thank you" and "I like your painting" or "good job," but "can I teach real talk?"

In this case, we see that real talk evolves through routines of social learning. It provides an important structure inherent in the learning process. Mary Pipher, in her book *The Shelter of Each Other*, reports a teacher as saying:

> "Kids today are missing some essential social skills for relating to each other. They don't know how to introduce themselves to other kids. They don't know how to negotiate or sustain a conversation. They relate to each other via put-downs. They're learning this from TV sitcoms. We can tell kids to be quiet and they just keep talking."

In response to a lack of skills, Pipher notes that a "vicious cycle" develops. "Teachers have unruly students, so they structure more, but that allows children even less interaction time. Students don't learn the interaction skills they need so they remain unruly. Then the teachers must structure even more." (Pipher, 1996, p. 76)

What Eileen demonstrates in her case is that teachers can use structure to teach the interaction skills that children so desperately need. Simply, interaction can be structured rather than eliminated. Eileen approaches the problem through both "instructional" and "situational" teaching. Both techniques are critical if we are to encourage real talk and social skill learning. When Eileen reads her children Mercer Mayer's *When I Get Mad* and then asks each of them what makes them mad, she is building on a practice of sharing. That is a part of her instructional technique. When one of her children suddenly does get upset, she seizes that emotional moment to acknowledge and discuss the immediacy of feeling, an example of situational teaching. When the children fuss over the play dough or can't figure out whose block ideas to use or how to take care of promises, she seizes a situation that can be crystallized into learning. "Ritual and Real" demonstrates that these structures provide skills that do in fact enable children to negotiate and sustain conversation.

It is often the benchmark of progress when, in fact, we do see the children use taught skills to negotiate a situation of their own making. Eileen notes that when real incidents occur, there is "real talk" if she responds to the unplanned moments. As Eileen goes on to say, "There have been many times in my teaching when I have ignored the obvious question for one that I had written in my plan book." Unfortunately (or fortunately) we cannot always prepare for the obvious questions. We can only hope we will take advantage of them as they occur.

At one point, Eileen watched one of her five year olds, a timid child, lead the morning greeting. In this ritual, a designated child walks from student to student saying good-morning, shaking each hand, uttering each name. This day the unexpected happened. There were several visitors in the room. With no prompting from the teacher, Jason walked over to them, said a loud and firm "good morning," and extended a gentle handshake while waiting for them to offer their names. His teacher wrote, "He had welcomed them to our classroom and I was so proud. As he took his place on the carpet next to me he looked at my beaming face and said, 'You sure look happy!'"

This case initially focused on the movement from ritual to real learning. It seems now that a more accurate map reveals moments of intersection between ritualized and real behavior. It is from this balance that children try out their voices, practice new phrases, share in the safety of the teaching circle and then in the independent interactions. Ritual is not fake. Real is not unpracticed or unschooled. Ritual and real, Eileen shows us, prepare and empower children to want to talk to each other, to want to make promises that they mean to keep.

CHAPTER FOUR

GETTING UNDERNEATH

Caring and Sharing Among Fives and Sixes

by Arona L. McNeill-Vann

Arona McNeill-Vann has been an educator for 19 years. Most of that time has been spent teaching young children between the ages of four and seven in private and public schools in the greater Washington, DC area. During the early 1980s, she took a sabbatical from early childhood education to work as a math resource teacher for adults with mental retardation. She later worked with two other teachers to develop a curriculum, "Cognitive Strategies for Survival Literacy," for adolescents with mental retardation.

For the past five years, Arona has been an early childhood cadre teacher for the DC school system. She has opened her classroom to visitors to observe *The Responsive Classroom®* practices in action. She has also presented workshops on *The Responsive Classroom®* and multi-age teaching.

In spring 1994, Arona and four colleagues wrote a proposal for a teacher-run school composed of multi-aged classes. Her colleagues chose her to be the lead teacher for The Nongraded School where she has taught since September of 1994. In September of 1995, The Nongraded School was designated an early childhood demonstration school for the DC Public School System.

Arona is married to Darryll Vann, who is also an early childhood teacher in the DC public school system. They have a son, McKissick, who is fourteen years old, and a black Lab named Myles.

"Oh, sorry."

How many times have you heard children give that automatic apology without any feeling behind it? Well, I've heard it a lot, and it really bothers me. For my case study, I chose to examine the issue of developing sincerity in children. My concern is that while it is easy to teach the language of respect and consideration, how do we get children to internalize the values behind the language?

WHY VALUES?

Why did I choose this case? Well, when I talk to parents about The Nongraded School and what makes us different from other schools, I usually talk about the difference between rote learning and real learning. In our school we want children to develop a real understanding of concepts such as addition and multiplication and to be able to discuss what they have read, as opposed to just repeating the words. I would like the same to hold true in the social curriculum. Given the young ages of my students, some of their learning is bound to be rote, but I think we, as adults, must try to help them even at four, five and six to begin to make certain values part of their nature.

Visiting parents sometimes comment on how friendly the children are in our school. I think this results directly from our attitudes about teaching values. If you want children to learn something, you have to teach them. This holds for values just as it does for reading and math. When social issues come up in the classroom, we take the time to deal with them. That's the goal, of course, but the challenge is making sure that how I deal with the issues encourages genuine feelings rather than lip service!

In teaching values I see my role as an "ethical coach," guiding my five and six year olds much as the outstanding Georgetown coach, John Thompson, guides his athletes. When he was interviewed about the possibility of his star player leaving college to go to the NBA, Thompson said that Allen Iverson was "not going anywhere, unless I tell him it's time for him to go." *(The Washington Post,* March 5, 1996) Later he clarified his comments by saying that, of course, Iverson would make the decision for himself, but that as a teacher and coach, it was his responsibility to give the young man as much guidance as possible, even though Iverson might not choose to follow that advice. What Thompson was saying about the responsibility parents and teachers have to give young people guidance is directly related to my desire to get beyond the language of respect to the values behind it. I believe teaching values is one of the most important roles a teacher has.

I recently ran across a column in the newspaper. Although I didn't agree with it in its entirety, one paragraph struck me as particularly true:

> The problem, of course, is that when "peaceful" behavior is learned by rote, it remains on the surface. Underneath, things can be seething. If the teacher doesn't deal with deeper problems such as peer group pressure, then all the trained mediators in the world won't succeed. . . .
> —Cheryl Benard, "Mediation Minus Morals,"
> *The Washington Post*, February 25, 1996

My goal through the case study was to find some ways to get underneath those surface behaviors while the children are still young.

My School

I teach in a magnet school which draws students from the entire Washington, DC area, although most live in Northwest Washington. The school, a teacher-run public school-within-a-school, serves children between four and ten years of age in multi-age classroom settings. This year we enrolled 85 students, including 83 African-American and two white children. Class sizes range from 12 to 20 with a full-time teaching assistant in each class. Because I also serve as the school administrator, my class this year has only twelve students, all five and six years old. Of those, ten are in my class for a second year. The two new students are both six year olds who have transferred from "traditional" DC public schools.

My Goals

Teaching in this setting helps me focus my objectives anew each year. This year, with the added incentive of the case study, I decided to focus on how I could help children begin to make the values of the social curriculum their own. To accomplish this, I planned to a) reflect on my behavior, asking myself frequently what I could do to encourage genuine respect while recognizing that everyone is not going to be liked equally by everyone else; b) model the desired behavior; and c) keep communication open with the children through regular class meetings.

As I thought about these goals I began to question what is developmentally realistic to expect from five and six year olds in terms of the social curriculum. While I knew that they weren't ready to show true altruism (most adults don't either), I believe that exposure to ideals should begin at an early age. As teachers, there are some things we really expect children to "learn" when we "teach" them but other times we give them experiences for the exposure or enrichment. I think some aspects of the social curriculum are like that. Maybe if we keep exposing children to genuine kindness, respect, and consideration and expect these things from them, the values will be understood and eventually internalized. I feel the same way about teaching Black history.

. . . how critical the language we use in the classroom is in laying the foundation for empathy. Just as children need a working knowledge of number concepts before they can memorize number facts, they need the language of respect and kindness in order to internalize the values behind the words.

Earlier in my career when I taught at Peabody and Watkins, another DC public school, I usually taught a few lessons on Mary McLeod Bethune. I chose her because both schools were within walking distance of Lincoln Park, which contains an impressive statue of Mrs. Bethune as well as a nice playground. Also, DC Public Schools has designated a week in May as Mary McLeod Bethune week. We would spend the week reading about her work as an educator and special advisor to President Roosevelt, and then we would visit the park. Of course, I didn't expect the children to memorize all the facts about Mrs. Bethune's life, but I thought that at least the next time someone mentioned her name, they would have a frame of reference. It worked, too! One year after our visit, we passed the park when we were on another field trip. One little girl said, "I just saw the statue of Mary McLeod Bethune!"

Ultimately, I want children to appreciate Mary McLeod Bethune's contributions, not just identify her statue. More than that, I want them to know that our city celebrates the black people who have made important contributions. Similarly, I want children to feel empathy for each other, not just say empty words, and I want them to understand why empathy is so important. How to achieve this in the social curriculum is the challenge.

SINCERITY AND LANGUAGE

Initially, I turned my attention to the issue of sincerity. I became concerned after a disappointing activity I had planned to help the children say good-bye to a classmate who was moving in the middle of the school year. On his last day in our class we planned to make Peter a book. Each child was given a page on which to write/draw "I like Peter because . . ." My assistant and I moved among the children, helping them with their writing. Maria was drawing, but she had not written any words. I asked if I could help her write what she wanted to say. She replied, "I can't think of anything to say." Simone then said, "That's not very nice!" I responded, "Well, Maria didn't say she didn't like Peter, she just said that she couldn't think of anything to say." I suggested that Maria continue to draw and maybe she would think of something. Later she came up and showed me what she had written, "I like Peter because he is cute." I was somewhat disappointed that was the best that she could do, but I didn't say anything. Most of the other children did not come up with deeply profound statements, but they wrote things like

"... he's my friend."
"... he's my best buddy."
"... he chases me on the playground. I will miss him."

In retrospect, it seemed like such a contrived situation because of the assumption that all children liked Peter, which may or may not have been true. Maybe a way to evoke more genuine feelings might have been to ask them to write about what they would remember about Peter.

This incident helped me realize how critical the language we use in the classroom is in laying the foundation for empathy. Just as children need a working knowledge of number concepts before they can memorize number facts, they need the language of respect and kindness in order to internalize the values behind the words. Substituting "what I will remember about Peter" for "what I like about Peter" would have allowed the children to reach out to another person in a way that was genuine. For a five or six year old, giving a book to a classmate who is leaving is an important first step in connecting to someone else. I needed to give them the language that would have allowed them to do this with sincerity.

The importance of language came to mind again when I was playing a lotto game with a small group of children. When it was time to clean up, I asked the children to pass me their playing cards. One little boy reached over the girl who was sitting next to me to hand me his card. She immediately said, "I don't like him!" When I asked her why, she said it was because she wanted him to pass the card to her so she could hand it to me. Again, I saw the importance of teaching them how to use respectful language. She needed to learn how to say, "I don't like what you did" instead of "I don't like you!"

SHARING

While struggling with ways to teach them to use respectful language with each other, I began to focus on the related issue of sharing because so much of the social curriculum at this age revolves around learning how to share. On reflection I realized that sharing was at the heart of my struggle to teach empathy and altruism. I wanted children to understand how to share a compliment, how to share friendship, and how to share their feelings. The book for Peter was really my attempt to help them share something very special with Peter—what they would remember about him. On the more concrete level, they needed to be able to share classroom materials. This issue arose in our classroom after some students had difficulty sharing a *Where's Waldo?* book that I had brought to school.

Several children were looking at it and more and more joined the group. After a while, Omari moved away from the group and went to read by himself, but he was obviously upset. I asked him what was wrong and he said that Zalika, who had gotten the book first, had told him that he could read with her, but then said he couldn't. When everyone had finished eating lunch, I called the class to the rug to discuss what had happened. Omari explained why he was upset. Zalika then responded in her somewhat magisterial tone that she had told him that he could not read with her because when it was Donte's turn to find Waldo, Omari had found Waldo first and, unable to contain his gleeful discovery, had pointed to him before Donte could take his turn. Anika, our new peace maker, then suggested that there should be a rule that no more than five people could read the Waldo book at a time.

Other children felt that everyone could share the book. They voted and eleven of the twelve children felt that they could share. Simone then suggested a round of apologies for hurt feelings and missed turns. So, all the apologies were made. I was particularly impressed that Simone was the one who suggested the apologies, since she was a child who sometimes appeared to be giving "lip service" to the language of *The Responsive Classroom.*® In this case, however, she seemed sincere in the role of facilitator.

The discussion then returned to the best way to share the book. One idea was to place the book in the middle of the group, so that everyone would be able to see it. Another suggestion was that "if you saw Waldo first and it was not your turn, you should keep it in your imagination" unless the person whose turn it was asked for help. Anika, the little girl who wanted to have the five people rule, then suggested that the class practice how to share the book, using their ideas (a role play!!). They then practiced placing the book so everyone could see and take turns finding Waldo.

The next day, when several children wanted to read the book, one child had trouble following the agreed-upon procedure. They talked to him, but that was not successful, so they came to me. I reminded him of the previous day's meeting and he then placed the book where everyone could see it. That same afternoon, Omari came to me because Anika was not sharing the book with him. I suggested that he remind her of the decision made by the class that the book should be shared with everyone. He went over to her, did so, and she let him have a turn. Class meetings and role playing were clearly strategies that worked well with this age group. I resolved to use them both more often.

Taking heart from the Waldo incident, I decided to give them more opportunities to practice sharing. I began by adapting an old ritual called "Pretzels" (Charney, 1992, p. 89) and substituting goldfish. In this ritual each child shares something another child has done. If the child's comment reflects appreciation, the commenting child gives the other child a goldfish. If not, the commenting child receives a goldfish from the other child. Remembering the difficulties we had experienced in creating the book for Peter, I wondered whether this would help children see each other in new ways. I hoped it would help them focus on specific behavior.

When I first began explaining the procedure, several children said that they did not want a turn, so I said that was all right. Once we started, however, everyone did participate. In fact, Maria, who originally did not want to participate, ended up giving away all of her goldfish. Some of the comments were:

"I liked watching you dance at the program."
"I liked when you read a book with me."
"I liked when you played with me."

The children did need reminders to focus on something specific that the person did rather than just saying, "I like Mary" or "Bobby is my friend." At first the children said only positive comments, but as the meeting went on they also expressed hurt feelings. Most of the negatives were directed at one child, Omari, but he listened to what was said and gave up his goldfish. I did feel rather uncomfortable about that and wondered if the activity would encourage Omari to share more or merely make him angry. The negatives focused mostly on sharing issues. By that time of year, most of the children in the class were six, so I guess it's not surprising that sharing, taking turns, and following rules were big social issues.

PLEASANT COLLABORATIONS

Sharing, empathy and altruism all seemed to be intricately entwined for this classroom of five and six year olds. How, as a teacher, could I help these young children develop greater empathy for their classmates? Contemplating my role as their ethical coach, I turned to research Abraham Maslow published about values and the self-actualized person. In his example of the student-teacher relationship, he said that the self-actualized teacher sees the relationship as a "pleasant collaboration" rather than as a clash of wills or authority. As the teacher gives up trying to be omniscient and omnipotent, "student-threatening authoritarianism" disappears from the classroom. The teacher no longer views the students as in competition with each other or with herself. According to Maslow, the self-actualized teacher's attitudes and values "create a classroom atmosphere in which suspicion, wariness, defensiveness, hostility, and anxiety tend to disappear. Threat responses tend to disappear in interpersonal situations when threat itself is reduced." (Maslow, 1970, p. 177) This was very helpful. For me, a big part of trying to develop an atmosphere of "pleasant collaboration" is remembering what behavior is developmentally appropriate for fives and sixes. This helps me encourage children to be sensitive to the feelings of others without resorting to threats or anger when they fail.

"Pleasant collaborations" defined quite nicely the kind of relationship I was seeking with children in my classroom, but I realized very quickly that it was not just with the children that I needed pleasant collaborations. I relied on those same kinds of collaborations with my colleagues, and several, in particular, helped me steer my program in new directions. Barbara Nophlin, a central administrator who provides instructional support to our school, met with me soon after I began experimenting with my variations on "Pretzels." She wondered whether the activity might cause children to focus too much on negative behavior. Since my goal was to encourage sharing/taking turns behavior, we decided that the activity should focus on positive, desired behavior.

At her suggestion, I paired children so that they could "catch" each other being friendly and I provided a reward that the partner could give to the "friendly" child at the end of the day. After all, it is not enough for adults to model the behavior; the children have to know how to identify the behavior in themselves and other children. Although it is harder for younger ones to look for specific behavior, Barbara thought that it might be important to focus on one or two kinds of behavior so we could dwell on the positive. We decided to focus on sharing and taking turns. After our meeting, I made a certificate the children could fill in and give to their partners if they observed them sharing.

A few days later, at the end of Morning Meeting, I announced that we were going to do a new activity. (I had already made a list of the partners for the day.) I explained that I had noticed that a lot of the arguments that people in our class were having were about sharing and taking turns. Today everyone would have a special job and their job was to observe their partner and remember a time during the day when the partner shared or took turns. I showed the certificate and explained that at the end of the day, if their partner had shared, they would get a certificate to fill out and give to their partner during our afternoon meeting. Anika asked if her partner had to share with her, and I said that the partner could share with anyone. For example, someone might share on the playground with someone from another class. I also gave an example of two children who were sharing a book before Morning Meeting.

Congratulations !!!

I noticed that Z a|i Kq

shared with me

today.

Omori   5 - 1 - 96
_{SIGNED}   _{DATE}

   That afternoon, I asked the children if they had observed their partners sharing during the day. Five of the twelve said yes. I gave them certificates to complete and when they were ready, I called the class to the rug. The children then presented the certificates to their partners, one at a time, and told the rest of us how the child had shared that day and with whom. We then clapped for all of the sharers and I said that I hoped that the next time everyone would get a certificate.

   Later that same week, we did the activity again, and nine children received certificates. Some children were better observers than others.

At least one child said that he did not see his partner sharing or taking turns that day, though I had observed the partner doing so. I felt, though, that I should not impose my observations, especially since I planned for the children to change partners each time we did the activity. My assistant and I also had partners so we could model the desired behavior. I decided to do the "catch your partner sharing" activity once or twice a week.

Barbara was able to come by one afternoon to observe the children awarding their sharing certificates. When we talked afterwards, she brought out the importance of having the children describe how their partner had shared to help them identify the desired behavior—"what it looks like," in Barbara's words. We had done this on other occasions and I agreed that it was a vital part of the activity and should be included all of the time.

At her suggestion I also began thinking about how the sharing certificates support the other aspects of a responsive classroom. If we want to have a school climate where children feel respected and part of the community, we (meaning the adults) have to incorporate activities into the school day which will facilitate that climate. The sharing activity helps children become aware of how their actions affect the feelings of others. It helps to develop their observational skills, and it is a way to acknowledge positive behaviors. It also means that the adults in the classroom are not the only ones who have the responsibility to "catch someone doing something good."

Barbara and I also discussed the academic skills which were a natural part of the activity. As the children completed a certificate, they wrote the name of their partner, the person the partner shared with, their own name, and the date. The children also read the certificate as they presented it. Here was a place where I charted real progress. By the time we did our last "catch your partner sharing" activity, the children included many more details in their observations. Examples were:

"I noticed that Zalika shared with me. She read a book with me."
"I noticed that Kwasi shared with Maria. They played mancala and took turns."
"I noticed that Anika shared with Jamar when they were playing on the playground."

Most of the children named times when their partner shared with them, but a few mentioned other children. At first, Mac said that he had not observed his partner (Anika) sharing. When Anika overheard him, she quickly reminded him of a time when she had shared, so everyone received a certificate!

Barbara asked me if I had seen any differences in behavior as a result of the "catch your partner sharing" activity. In the classroom it is often difficult to attribute a behavior, especially a social one, to a specific activity. One day, however, a child made a comment which may have been the direct result of our focus on sharing. I was reading *Anansi the Spider* by Gerald McDermott with a group of six children. In the story Anansi has six sons, each with a different talent. When Anansi gets into trouble, each son uses his particular skill to help rescue his father. After the rescue Anansi finds a "beautiful globe of light" in the forest and says he will give it to the "son who rescued me." The problem is, since all six helped with the rescue, which son deserves the prize? During our discussion, one of the children very quickly responded that the sons should share the prize. In fact, that is what happens in the story. Anansi cannot decide who should get the prize, so Nyambe, the god of the Ashanti people, takes the globe of light and puts it in the sky for "all to see" at night. I like to think that our classroom focus on sharing made his solution an obvious one to everyone.

Brenda Clark, another colleague with whom I discussed my case study, suggested that I read *You Can't Say You Can't Play* by Vivian Paley as it relates directly to the ideas of sharing and empathy. It really is a compelling book. In some ways it reminded me of the comment by John Thompson—that we as the significant adults in the children's lives have certain responsibilities to fulfill. We do have an obligation to provide moral direction though we recognize that ultimately these children will not be going into a perfect world. I think that most teachers are generally optimists who believe that perhaps if they can instill kindness and empathy in children at an early age, the children will carry those qualities with them as adults.

Two passages in the book convinced me that I should implement the "You can't say you can't play" rule in my classroom next year as a way to reinforce my other notions of empathy and sharing:

. . . although we all begin school as strangers, some children never learn to feel at home, to feel they really belong. They are not made welcome enough. (Paley, 1992, p. 103)

. . . each time a cause for sadness is removed for even one child, the classroom seems nicer. (Paley, 1992, p. 95)

The second passage is the one which helped me to give up the notion that an individual should have the right to choose his or her playmates at school. This truly is an instance when the needs of the community must carry more weight than the needs of the individual. Of course, this then raises the question of whether individuals really have a "need" to exclude or whether this is a learned behavior.

The conversations that Paley had with the older children at her school also helped to convince me to start using the rule. They said that you have to teach this when the children are young and still willing to accept it, and that many of their worst memories of school were when they were in kindergarten or first grade and were excluded. When I talked with the oldest students in my school (eight to ten year olds), they, too, thought that it would be hard to enforce the "You can't say you can't play" rule with older children. The one child who did think that the rule would be a good idea for the whole school is one who has trouble making friends and is often excluded by her peers.

Barbara and I discussed my decision to use the "You can't say you can't play" rule. She seemed a little surprised so I told her about the Waldo book class discussion. In that instance, the children decided that they had to share with everyone. I might be reading more into that than the children intended, but weren't they telling me something then? If the rule makes sense for the Waldo book, then why not for all activities? And if not for all activities, where do I draw the line? It seems to me that it is a lot more complicated, confusing, and perhaps even hypocritical, to say to children, "These are the times when we must include everyone, and these are the times when it is OK to exclude others."

The children in my class have proven to me that they are able to take another's point of view, at least some of the time, as evidenced by the discussion and resolution of how to share the Waldo book. For five and six year olds, sharing and taking turns is a most appropriate way to demonstrate empathy. This was their first step outward towards understanding not just the feelings of others, but how those feelings affect the group as a whole. Perhaps even more important, they've shown me that sometimes they can choose the needs of the larger community over their own. They have also shown that when given the opportunity, they can figure out how to solve problems and they can observe and acknowledge sharing behavior in their peers. The case studies as a group confirmed my belief that children must be a part of the process of resolving issues that arise in the classroom. I continue to be impressed by the sometimes sophisticated and sensitive thinking of my students.

On the other hand, I have always felt that the first teachers of a child have a powerful role in that child's development. We as teachers may not be able to change the entire world, but maybe we can make the world of school a place where all children feel comfortable and protected. The stories of the other case studies reinforce my belief that we can and should set high moral standards for children of all ages. The teacher does have a responsibility to be a moral coach. The teacher must be confident and secure about the values that she wishes to instill in her students and must practice the desired behaviors in her interactions with children and adults alike.

My clear positive at the beginning of the case study was for children to begin to make the values of the social curriculum their own. In the case of my five and six year old students, this means that they will share materials and take turns. They will speak to others in a respectful tone of voice. They will establish and follow rules for the classroom. They will use words to solve problems and resolve conflicts. They will take pride in themselves and their school.

Next year I plan to add "You can't say you can't play" to the Golden Rule in my classroom. I believe that fours and fives, with my guidance, will be able to understand why the two rules belong together. My goal is to establish a climate where all children feel protected and where there is a "pleasant collaboration" between students and teacher. I want my school to be a place where all children feel safe, secure, and have a sense of belonging.

Having the structure of the case study forced me to be disciplined in my reflections on my educational philosophy and practice. The act of writing down my thoughts has helped to clarify some issues for me, although that doesn't mean that I have been able to come up with neat little answers. The writing process, though, helped me focus on language, which ultimately became an important element in my thinking and teaching.

The case study also caused me to look at a variety of sources as I contemplated my concerns. I returned to the writings of Maslow and found a new resource in Vivian Paley. I initiated several conversations with colleagues around the issue of teaching values, and through such dialogues, developed a sharing activity which I feel meets the developmental needs of my students while nurturing the growth of sincerity and sensitivity to the needs of others. Finally, I am now comfortable with my responsibility to teach certain basic human values such as kindness, consideration, and sincerity.

RUTH'S COMMENTARY *Getting Underneath*

"I want my children to begin to make the values of the social curriculum their own. Such a simple statement for such a big challenge!"

—Arona McNeill-Vann

Arona describes the class making a book to give as a present to a classmate who is leaving. Maria can't think of something to say. "That's not nice," Simone chimes in. Here is one of those incidents, fairly common, easily overlooked, that I find mean so much. It is easy for me to see how it sparked the many questions embedded in this case study.

How do we balance the needs of the community with the needs of the individual?

Two thoughts occur to me. One thought concerns the issue of task expectations. All children are expected to add a page to the book—it is not a choice activity. In fact, Arona returns to Maria and prods a response until Maria produces something, even if it is, according to the teacher, "a disappointment." Second, I would like to look at the presumption that this is a "contrived situation" because of the expectation that children will all come to like each other. This appears an important handle on the problem of fake versus sincere and offers insight into how we may teach children to understand the values beneath the gestures.

All students are expected to participate in the book task. Certainly, another way to do this would be to let children decide if they had a page they wanted to contribute. Yet Arona gives each one a page. There is, I feel, an assumption here that begins to define community. In expecting Maria's participation, I believe that Arona is establishing a concept of the classroom as a community. Maria perseveres because she accepts Arona's expectation, but she is also learning that she has a role in the community. She has something to say to her classmates.

How and when to require participation are among the key decisions that teachers make. These decisions have implications for the way children come to understand their part in community. When, for example, there is a choice to take part in discussion, the same hands regularly shoot up. The loudest, most vocal, most confident will often dominate—not just one discussion or one Morning Meeting but many. And others, perhaps more quiet or reserved by temperament, opt out. Some tune out, withdrawing into daydreams or diversionary play. Others are perhaps more selective, a good audience when the topic or the presenter appeals to them. Responsibility then is individualistic and topical. There is little accountability to community and to the rules, the rituals and the members, to an obligation that overrides oneself.

When Arona expects everyone to contribute a page, she assumes that communal interest. This is not to say that there isn't the reality of preference and selectivity. We all listen more keenly to some stories than to others. We all listen more readily to some speakers than to others. And we often fail to listen and learn through others because of our discriminatory filters. We can cause damage because we shut down or tune out. The willingness to listen to another's point of view and to heed the stories of those we call strangers allows respect and finally empathy to develop. When we let ourselves or our children select and prejudge, we narrow and restrict their ability to learn community. We see the question of how to balance individual with community needs come up again and again in Arona's case study: while sharing Waldo, during "catch your partner sharing" and in the decision not to allow exclusion during play. Again, every time we decide to make sharing a rule of the room, inclusion an expectation, we are saying something about the value and nature of community. When we permit our children to say, "I don't want to do that," we say something about respect for individual needs and differences. The question is never one or the other. The question is how to achieve a balance so that we develop and teach the privileges of belonging and the significance of individual worth.

How do we help children "know" each other?

Thinking about the book-making activity, Arona writes, "In retrospect, it seemed like such a contrived situation, because of the assumption that all the children liked Peter, which may or may not have been true." She goes on to say that perhaps if she had worded the task differently and asked them about memories, she would have generated more genuine feelings. This "simple" jump from like to remembering jostled my thinking. It is not a mere switch of vocabulary; it is a giant stride forward in meaning. We so often like what we know and understand. We like what engages us. We like those we play, laugh and eat with, those we talk with, those we know best. Before we like, we must know. And to know . . . well, to know means to notice, to share Waldo books, to share jump rope games, to share in the life of the classroom.

This is "a simple statement" but so complex. I see it over and over. If the task had changed, would Maria have quickly called to mind a memory? Perhaps and perhaps even in this small group of twelve she would have recalled nothing. We do allow children to be invisible to each other, to share space and endless hours without a conversation or an interaction. There are diverging interests, clashing temperaments and plain old dislikes that wedge us apart, but in addition there is the unknown. One of my eighth grade students recently described it in a way that truly struck me. "No one recognizes me," she said. "I dress differently. I like different things than most of you. I know that. But what feels bad is that no one ever seems to recognize me." What does she mean? How much meaning is in this blunt statement? Part of what I hear is not the demand to be liked, but the wish to be noticed and known.

When we move from asking children to like each other to asking children to "observe" and notice each other, we create an opportunity for genuine liking to emerge. This is what I understand James Baldwin to mean when he says, "No one, after all, can be liked whose hu-

man weight and complexity cannot be, or has not been, admitted."
(Baldwin, 1955, p. 161) To be recognized is to add your weight to the
community. And to be recognized in your complexity is to get past the
labels of "boy" or "bad" or even "friend" to have detail and description: "He chases me on the playground. I will miss him."

This, I believe, redirects the interventions—the focus that switches
from prescriptions "of liking" to the active task of observation. It is
developmentally realistic for the fives and sixes. It also realizes what
Arona states is the need to use language properly to lay "the foundation for empathy."

As they decide how to read *Where's Waldo?* together, the children
generate a sharing rule and a way to organize that sharing that reflects
an ability to observe. They notice when turns are skipped, ignored, or
monopolized. They vote to share. The rule that everyone must see,
which becomes part of their procedure, is very much like the idea that
everyone must be seen. The subsequent activities that Arona introduces
continue to build on their ability to notice. She helps children see and
articulate the particulars, the complexities that give human weight. In
addition, she helps children notice the positive sides of sharing.

What techniques can support this process?

In this teaching process there occurs both instructional and situational
learning. "Catch your partner sharing" is an example of instructional
learning. The teacher invents an activity and puts it in place to direct
children in their learning. She instructs them in the use of a language
pattern, "I noticed that . . ." and provides a certificate to reinforce the
language and the action. A ceremony completes the process, again
within the structure of specific language and actions. The teacher
models first. Students model for each other. The weekly repetition
quickly shows the rapid learning that occurs in this group as the ability to notice improves and as children improvise to fill gaps.

The skirmish over the Waldo book provides an opportunity for situational learning. Arona neither ignores nor mandates here but she does
intervene. She first intervenes by observing an upset student. She takes
time to find out why he is hurt and then takes more time to have a class
discussion. We can see that this is not the first class discussion ever to occur. There is certainly acceptance of a problem and a willingness to try

to find a solution. Several children offer ideas. One is voted on by the class and given very concrete procedures, steps established by the children. It is situational because the teacher seizes a particular situation and turns it over to the class so that they can construct a solution.

What is the role of the teacher?

The role of the teacher looms large here. The movement from fake to sincere and from ritual to real becomes more and more feasible through the attentive efforts of the teacher to notice, to revise, to channel and to collaborate. It is thus essential that Arona defines her own authority and purpose. "We as teachers may not be able to change the entire world, but maybe we can make the world of school a place where all children feel comfortable and protected." The teacher becomes in Arona's words "an ethical coach" not from a stance of omnipotence, but in a role of "pleasant collaboration." Her willingness to guide children, to welcome them, to remove "a cause for sadness," to help them develop respect and goodness, gains strength as the case study progresses. And as I reread it, I wonder if it is because the case study offers some irrefutable evidence about their social needs, evidence that intertwines the teacher in the social learning of her children.

When teachers share with each other, everyone benefits. As Arona confers with her colleagues, she hones her ideas, improves her strategies to help children grow, and gathers evidence and ideas to direct future changes. As teachers share more with each other they too gather the courage of their convictions.

CHAPTER FIVE

LETTING THE SPILL GROW

Conflict Resolution in a First Grade

by Linda Mathews

Linda Mathews has spent fourteen years teaching in grades six, three, and one—including twelve years in the first grade. She received both her B.S. and M.S. degrees from Southern Connecticut State University. Named Connecticut State Teacher of the Year in 1991, Linda is in *Who's Who Among America's Teachers,* is a cadre teacher for *The Responsive Classroom,*® and is a teacher author for *Math 1* (Saxon Publications). Married to William Mathews, Linda has two children—Dr. Shannon Mathews-Martinello and William B. Mathews.

One day several colleagues came into my classroom to observe the children as they were creating projects. As we walked around the room I heard the voices of two students escalate. They were working on wintry projects in which glitter was featuring prominently. One of the students had been prone to impulsive actions when faced with a problem so I moved closer to the area where they were having their discussion. Glitter covered the table. Greg was explaining, "I did my project and I was just trying to get the sparkles into the sparkle box." Katie, clearly exasperated, wailed, "There are sparkles all over the table!" Both faces turned to me to intervene. I asked them how they were going to solve this problem. After some discussion, they decided to work together to sweep up the twinkling desktop. I could easily see that the problem was solved and the mess was rapidly disappearing. So why was I so annoyed? Was I just embarrassed because colleagues were watching? That certainly contributed to my feelings of disquiet, but I was also upset because once again the children had seemed to need my intervention to solve their problem.

I begin each year with two social goals for my twenty-seven first graders. I want them to be able to solve conflicts with their classmates in a peaceful and respectful manner and I want them to be able to do it without my intervention. Early in September I introduce them to a conflict resolution process called SETS, an acronym for:

Stop and get cool.
Explain what you are unhappy about.
Talk at the table.
Shake hands.

Together we practice these techniques so the children can learn to use them on their own. We also work at community tables with shared crayons, scissors, and pencils. This gives them ample opportunities to practice sharing. Often we engage in cooperative learning activities and group-building games so the children can develop a better sense of how to relate to others in the classroom. After one or two months the children usually seem quite comfortable following our rules and settling their difficulties on their own or at the conflict resolution table.

So I puzzled why, in spite of all these arrangements, some children still persisted in their need to check in with me before trying to resolve their problems. As I looked in dismay at the glitter-spangled table, I couldn't help thinking of the many children who were still barraging me daily with "Mrs. Mathews, so and so is doing such and such." I know that six year olds are ready to begin solving many kinds of problems without my assistance. Faced with this glittering December disappointment, I decided it was time to try to understand why some children always begin by seeking my help rather than initiating conflict resolution themselves. This was to be my case study.

I began by examining my classroom. The children come from a fairly stable, somewhat homogeneous community. Many were probably accustomed to having their parents solve their problems for them. I thought about the developmental needs of the children. They ranged in age from six to eight years old. At this age, children often have a tendency to be competitive, impulsive, and somewhat egocentric, factors I would have to keep in mind. I considered how the physical set-up of the room might be contributing to the problem. I wondered, did our work at community tables with shared supplies help reinforce the notion that everyone needed to work together in respectful ways? I examined whether the cooperative learning activities and group-building games were actually establishing a greater sense of cohesiveness. Mostly, I focused my thoughts on the conflicts which children could not seem to solve without first asking for my intervention. For the remainder of December I recorded each conflict in a journal.

In January I read through a collection of these journal entries and examined some of my own responses to the children. I began to see some patterns. First, my own voice dominated discussions. I could see that I needed to give the students more opportunities to practice directing their own moves. I decided to keep a tally of the number of times I interjected my thoughts into a situation without first giving ample time for the students to solve the situation by themselves. In incident after incident, I also observed children who knew the appropriate language to use—children who had role played and practiced how to solve problems—fail to use that language. I was perplexed by this situation.

Reflecting about some of my journal entries, I suddenly thought back to what I had once learned in a workshop on teaching: *begin with the children.* So many times I find myself wrestling with questions and decisions that affect my teaching and I wrestle alone. I needed to begin by discussing the problem with those who would be most affected by my decisions. I decided to ask the children how they felt about our problem solving to see what solutions they would suggest. I wanted them to be more responsible, so I needed to allow them to take responsibility for this particular problem.

THE MEETING

On a winter Monday morning we assembled at the rug for a "Talk it Out" meeting. I posed my problem to the group.

Me: I was wondering what you have noticed about how we have
    been solving problems in our classroom.
Alison: We talk our problems out.
Joseph: We use SETS.
Robbie: Sometimes we come to you and get help.
Teresa: We go to the table and talk it over.
Me: I have noticed that some of you come to me and tell me
    about the problem first and some of you try something out
    on your own. Why do you think that is?

There was quiet in the circle and I sensed that the wheels were
turning.

Erin: Some of us aren't mad too much and we can talk it out.
    When you're really mad you might need someone big to
    help you calm down.
Deirdre: My mother says to go to a grown-up and get help.
Katie: Sometimes the problems are little and they can be made
    smaller by yourself. Sometimes they aren't.
Me: You are telling me about having little problems and big
    problems. Can you explain what a big problem or a little
    problem is?

Hands shot up all around the circle as I walked over to the chart
stand to record the responses.

Me: First tell me about what you mean when you tell me that
    there are little problems. Can you give me some examples?

We developed the following list:

Small Problems
If I need a pencil.
When I don't have any paper.
If I need some space.
Sometimes the bathroom is messy.
I lose something.
When I don't have a snack.
I am speaking and I need people to listen.

Me: Now, can you give me some examples of big problems?

Big Problems
Cutting me in line.
Fighting.
Pushing.
Someone takes your things.
When stuff isn't fair.

When the list was completed we took a break. We gathered together again about twenty minutes later. We read the Small Problems and Big Problems lists again. I directed the following question to the group:

Me: I was wondering, you gave me a list of problems that you felt were little and problems that you felt were big. What do you think is the difference between a little problem and a big one?
Seamus: Your friends can help you with the little problems.
Patrick: The little problems aren't scary.
Alison: You can figure out what to do with the little problems. You can't figure out what to do with the bigger problems.
Mary Ellen: You're mad with the big problems and not mad with the little ones.
Frankie: Little problems are just little, you know, easy.
Me: So you are telling me that a little problem is one you feel you can solve yourself and with a big problem it might feel scary and you might not know what to do?

The heads nodded yes.

Anthony *(in a most excited voice):* But we do, we do have a way to get calm and not feel scary. You see, we already have SETS and in my karate class I learned how to stay calm and not feel scared. I learned how to "rotate." *(At this point he assumed a lotus like position with arms out, fingers pinched together and legs crossed.)* If you do that and breathe in your mouth and out through your nose then the big stuff isn't so scary. So maybe if we "rotate" first and then go to do SETS, things won't feel scary.

After explaining that many people call that technique meditation we all closed our eyes and practiced.

> Sara: Why don't we show a friend this sign if we are scared or mad? *(Sara gestured with her hands.)*
>
> Anthony: That's what I said, things don't feel scary.
>
> Me: That's a solution that would be a place to start when we are faced with the big problems. What do you do when you need to solve a little one?
>
> Andrew: Well, if the bathroom is messy, you just go up and ring the bell, wait until everyone looks at you and then you tell the kids about it. Someone comes to clean it up and you get your turn.
>
> Me: Does anyone have another way of solving a small problem by yourself?
>
> Ron: If someone lost their pencil and they already tried to find it, they could check out the lost and found and then ask their team to help them. If you don't find a pencil there then you go to another team and ask.

Felicia and Jay were having a problem keeping their feet walking in a safe way on the way back from lunch. They talked about how they could walk together in a careful way. The next two days, after their talk, they walked so safely! Wow.

Me: So it seems that you have special things to do that help you solve the little problems. *(Heads nod yes.)* Some days it seems to me that you come to me first and ask for help solving problems, big or little. You seem to know what to do by yourselves. Why do you think that you come to me first?

Jimmie: To tell you what happened.

Katie: So you can solve the problem quickly.

Sara: You can get help so you won't get mad at each other.

Me: It seems to me that you already know what to do to solve the little problems. What can we give you to do when you are faced with a problem you can't seem to solve by yourself?

Jimmie: We could write about it. Then we could look at it to see what to try.

Lucia: We could try to remember what to do by ourselves.

Michael: We could go get a friend to listen to our problem and help us.

The conversation went on until we had put into place some specific techniques to use for solving a problem. We decided to have a notebook where children could write about the problems they solved. They could also use a piece of paper from this book to write to a friend about a problem they wanted to discuss. We assigned two children to be "listening friends." These children would act as mediators if a group of children could not arrive at a solution. (There would be modeling and role playing provided so children could practice being a listener in the near future.)

After experiencing this discussion, I felt like I had attended a conflict resolution workshop. I was allowed to be a witness to the insights and feelings of the children.

My observations:

- Children felt that they had some specific skills in place to use when faced with a problem. When they felt secure about what to do they labeled the problem "little."
- Children recognized that some problems felt small and some problems felt scary.
- Children experienced a "scary feeling" when they encoun-

tered a "big problem." They did not know what to do to solve big problems.

- Children needed to have a plan of action in order to begin resolving conflicts independently.
- Children needed to feel that there were friends and adults there to listen when a problem felt overwhelming.
- Children always need to be part of the process. Always begin with them.

This meeting gave me a wonderful beginning. We quickly introduced two new interventions as a result of our class discussion—we established class mediators and we started our *We Are The Problem Solvers* book in which children could record their conflict and its resolution, illustrate the page and read the description to the class. But problems are rarely so simple that they can be solved in just one or two discussions. I wanted to understand this problem in its full complexity so I shared my concerns with my colleague Colette who teaches fifth grade in my school.

Colette and I have been friends for many years. We share the same philosophy about teaching and often encounter each other at system-wide meetings. We rarely see each other at school because students of different grade levels occupy different wings of the building. This project has given us some time together to share thoughts and feelings. One afternoon we discussed how the need to be recognized influences children's actions in the classroom. I shared my concerns with Colette about how my first graders were approaching conflict resolution. She asked if one reason might be because the child needed to be recognized. We have a time for representing, a show shelf, sharing time, greetings and farewells every day. But perhaps this was not enough. Were the children coming to me with their small concerns because they needed to be recognized in some way? I thought about why some children might need this teacher connection. When Erin came to me to report that she needed a pencil (the routine already having been well established for getting a pencil), she seemed to be telling me that she needed to touch base:

Erin: Mrs. Mathews, I can't do my Writer's Workshop story because I don't have a pencil.

PETER WRENN

Me: Can you think of what you might do when your team is
   out of pencils?
Erin: Go to another team and ask if they have one for me?
Me: That's something to try.

Erin was immediately off, glancing back to me during the jaunt to the
next table.

What I try now with Erin is to give her recognition throughout the
day—a smile, a pat on the back, a short conversation about her projects. When I go to her more often, I see a reduction in the times she
needs to come to me to make that connection. Many of the students
already have become more adept at developing conflict resolution skills
and knowing where to begin since our meeting about big and little
problems. The children who are still coming up to me are children
who seem to exhibit young traits in many areas and may be seeking
out a little added security by touching base with me. Am I onto something here?

Recently, Colette and I began to look at when these requests for
help in conflict resolution were occurring. What activities were my students engaged in at the time? Were they engaged enough in what they

were doing? Were problems solved in a quicker fashion when the children wanted to get on with their work? These are questions well worth pursuing, but they'll have to wait until next year.

When I began this project I said I wanted children to be more responsible. I have thought about this idea a great deal and I find myself coming back to one theme—that of self-reliance. In this uncertain world where families, support systems, and social mores are always in a state of flux, I want children to know what to do when conflicts arise. I want them to make choices that will be healthy for them. I want them to try out successful strategies when they are six and seven so that they will have resources within themselves and/or people they can turn to when they must face choices with heavier consequences in the years ahead. Focusing my attention on this problem has helped me see children's needs that I had missed earlier. When I record activities and procedures children are using to complete tasks successfully, I begin to see evidence that my efforts have not been in vain:

> Anthony upsets his juice glass while unpacking his backpack. "Would somebody help me with this?" he says while walking toward the sink. Seamus goes to his assistance and sponges and brown paper towels fly across the floors and table tops. For a moment the spill seems to expand in size but as I watch it grow, the "spill team" gets the job done. In years past, my first reaction would have been to step in and help Anthony clean the mess quickly and efficiently. Now I stand back, keep my motherly impulses in check and allow the children to handle the situation. I am duly rewarded.

> Alison is sharing a painting of a forsythia branch she made during choice time. During comment and question time, Robbie

tells her that he likes her picture. I wait for Alison's response. So often before I would have stepped in and said, "Robbie, you need to tell Alison what you like about her picture." Alison handles the situation with ease, simply asking, "Why?" Robbie replies, "It really looks like forsythia in the yellow parts."

In math we ask the children to work with a partner and measure the width of the classroom using their own feet as a unit of measure. One student walks the line, foot to heel, foot to heel, until he reaches the other side of the room. This requires a great deal of balance. We decide, after some discussion, that everyone will walk with a friend who will hold them up and then reverse roles. Each team will record its findings on the chart for class discussion later. After a few children have modeled how to do this, the group disperses. Joseph and Delia are partners. She begins to walk with her hand on Joseph's shoulder. About a third of the way across she stops. "You're wiggling and I can't walk straight," she says in a crisp voice. Joseph looks at her and with a slight smile replies, "No, I'm not." I watch as Delia stands her ground and takes in a quick breath. She then walks to the problem solving table and waits. Joseph stands alone to consider his retort. After a minute or two, he slowly walks over and they begin to talk. I overhear phrases such as, "When it's your turn do you want me to do that to you? How would you feel?" "Well, your fingers were diggin' into me." They continue to talk, then record how they solved their problem in the book and return to work. They wrote: "We wer waking dirin math. Joseph let me go. Mi fingers hurted him. We are guna uze a switsurt on mi arm." Was Delia upset? Yes. Did she have a plan of action? She did. The problem was dealt with. Feelings were shared. They got back to work.

While corresponding with Ruth during the evolution of this case study she helped me to see certain steps emerging from the processes we went through together in the classroom. One of the most important times we spent together was when we sat as a class and began to discuss the fact that we had problems to solve in the classroom. We noticed that we had difficult situations and recognized that we needed to discuss what would happen when these situations would arise. *Step one is to identify or name the problem.*

After naming our concern, we began to go through a process which defined the different levels of problems we faced. When we had the discussion about big and little problems it became very apparent to me that there were times when the children felt that they could face a problem on their own and times when they felt that they could not. *Step two is to narrow the problem.* In our class we asked, "Is it big or small?"

What do you do if you are confronted with a big problem or a little one? All the children needed to have a plan of action in place to help them resolve the problem they faced. *Step three is to give children strategies to use.* We did this by providing a place to calm down, modeling ways to "get calm" (Anthony's rotation technique), giving students the chance to explain their viewpoint, allowing children time to talk about their dilemma, and letting children know that they could attempt solutions on their own.

> I changed a lot this year. One way I grew up was—
>
> that I didn't fight over the pensal

What if the problems being faced are big ones? What if the child cannot figure out what to do on his/her own? I want students to have techniques or a network of people to go to when they get stuck. Our social studies curriculum includes a unit of study called Personal Safety. Within this unit there is an activity which suggests that you brainstorm a list of people children can go to when they have a problem. We came up with a list of over twenty people. The list ranged from the familiar parent to the unknown hotline operator but we had places to go when things got scary.

CONCLUSION

Do you have a vision of me sitting in my chair and recording conflict resolutions all day as the children move from task to task? (I didn't even know there was a chair for me in my classroom.) Sitting is an art that teachers get to practice only while driving to and from work. So what is my place now that we have begun to pinpoint specific techniques and steps to follow when conflicts arise?

Big problems still overwhelm children. They may still need my help as Robbie and Nick so clearly described: "We got into a fight. Robbie and me were playing and I bumped into Nick. He said 'watch it'—then we were fighting—what could we do?"

Young children must have adults available when their own controls break down. We must be willing to help. Conflict resolution is an ongoing process. I see my place as one where I

I changed a lot this year. One way I grew up was-
to rey snackt the pesin how is specking.

am available when children don't know what to do. I am here to remind them of strategies to try. I might have to bring them to the group and have them elicit suggestions from their friends. I am here to model. I am here to listen. I am here to give a hug or do the "Happy Dance" with Sean when he is faced with an especially grumpy day. We are all here to try to work things out together. The numerous requests for help solving the "Mrs. Mathews so and so is . . . " problems have drastically been reduced. We now face more complex issues together. When I need help clarifying and rethinking classroom situations, I go to the children. Have we grown together this year? I think so. As one child wrote in our *We Are The Problem Solvers* book, "We had a priam. We sol it. it waz harde but we bid it."

They were right. We had a problem. We solved it. It was hard, but we did it.

RUTH'S COMMENTARY *Letting the Spill Grow*

I am reminded that children are best prepared to care for themselves and others when they feel cared for by the adults in their lives. As I read this case, I think about the journey towards self-reliance. I think about the continual rhythm of holding and releasing, of boundaries that offer the confidence to explore and the promise of adventure that must be part of that journey. I think about the spills, the spill team and the deliberate problem solving in Linda Mathews' first grade classroom. I see all the work that helps children along the way. Often we think that everything is in place for a great program to work and yet the children don't use it. In this case, we see a teacher who looks for what is missing rather than giving up or saying that her children cannot do it.

Although Linda Mathews' study is focused on aspects of self-reliance, it is important not to lose sight of the careful balance of structure and autonomy that she creates in this classroom. Why do I find myself coming back to this issue over and over? Why do I insist on pointing out the structures that underlie student participation, whether in the choices of their classroom (Kaplan and McCaffrey), real talk (Mariani), play fighting (Jacques), or sharing (McNeill-Vann)? Isn't it obvious that children learn to rely on inner resources through hard work? Yet some theoreticians continue to think that if the teacher will just stop intervening and stay out of the way, children will start to solve their own problems, even if their first attempts are a bit messy, a bit ugly, quarrelsome and mean. What I understand as I read this case is just how important all those steps are that provide for the student/teacher collaboration, and the construction of a structure that truly nurtures autonomy.

Twenty-plus years ago when I faced my first classroom of first graders, I expected children to make many choices in the classroom. I had observed as a student teacher many classrooms where active learning and student-initiated activities flourished. I saw children map their city, research bridges, investigate tunnels, write stories and compare, argue, share and come to understand through the richness of peer and teacher interactions. I took all that into a public school in

Harlem. And at first, my translation of that process was a wreck. But somehow I learned to make it work and began to see that it was possible to teach the more hidden skills, largely the skills of self-discipline. Then my students, too, mapped neighborhoods, constructed wonderful dioramas, engaged in vocal and purposeful conversations, initiated and problem-solved. I observed that it was possible for children to learn the particular cognitive and social skills they would need to work effectively in a more student-centered classroom. They learned when I learned how to teach those skills in the same systematic ways in which I was helping them learn to read.

Linda Mathews' case study illustrates a way that her students develop the self-reliance to solve many real and lively problems. Her case demonstrates the use of tools and strategies which help both teacher and child gain confidence. Moving from setting up a classroom table for problem-solving to creating actual problem-solvers is a sometimes tiring route; yet with persistence and understanding we see the accomplishment. Importantly, so does their teacher. In the spring, Linda records in her classroom journal so much that works. A child gets quiet when asked to by another child. An orange juice spill is wiped up. A reminder to tidy up passes from peer to peer—nicely!!! The group moves over to make room for one more person on the rug. Children listen to each other. Children respond with appropriate actions. And children identify and assert what they need—a place in the circle, a bit more quiet, help with a spill, a reason for liking the picture, a steady hand with a math problem. Every one of these moments—every one of these small and typical exchanges—might have gone awry. For each one that was settled with friendly words and respectful gestures, a better day was achieved.

"I want children to be able to solve problems without coming to me," Linda writes as she initiates this case. She is clearly frustrated. Although a solid structure is already in place to help children solve problems (SETS), the children keep coming to the teacher first. In their version of the process step one is to complain to the teacher. When redirected, they show that they do know how to begin to use the strategies they have; yet they don't use them—at least that is what Linda observes. After the annoyance and dust settles, Linda realizes that there must be some pieces missing. Sixes, she knows, are at a developmental stage where they need to be seen. A first grade room is one without barriers that occlude a teacher's visual field. Hidden corners invite testing and mischief. Tension, at this age, is often expressed by increased demands for teacher attention. "Look at this." "Teacher come here." "Teacher, know what Ronnie just did?" The tugs, yanks, and tattling can be a maddening wake up call. Something is not right.

Linda records several important breakthroughs during the year. The first occurs when the students are invited to name the problem. Linda calls them to a meeting and asks what they have noticed. They lump problems into two categories of Big and Little. The bigger problems entail more emotional risk, more anger ("when stuff isn't fair"; "someone takes your things"). The class is able to generate a number of strategies to use when confronted with the scary problems. They are able to recognize all the non-scary problems. In fact, many of the conflicts they seem to take care of without teacher intervention are the little ones. I wonder if the distinction frees them to act more readily. Permission is given to get help with bigger problems, peer and teacher help. Clarifying the notion that it is good to stop and to "get calm" when something goes wrong is also a way to reinforce the distinctions between little and big, safe and less safe situations. The children should gain ease and confidence as they practice handling the little problems, a useful rehearsal for the bigger, scarier ones.

A second breakthrough is generated by the techniques of practice. In one episode, Linda describes a dispute that erupts over some spilled glitter. It is not unusual for things to spill and yet the teacher is somewhat provoked. She knows that her sixes, speedy, often clumsy and reckless, are to be expected to spill. Clearly, her solution is not to banish glue, glitter, paint, juices and everything else that pours, tumbles and drips. The solution is to teach children how to clean it up. In this case, with reinforcement and redirection the children figure out their job. So what is the problem? Why does Linda linger over this episode? Perhaps because there are other teachers observing in the room. Or perhaps because of a certain ambivalence on the part of the teacher. Does she need to intervene? Again, we know that Linda wants her children to be able to solve problems without her assistance. She wants them to know how to clean up the glitter and how to figure out the fault-finding and the job delegation without her having to be there. In this case, the children are not ready to take care of both phases. Soon they will be.

Next it becomes important for the teacher to stand back and give the children the opportunity to practice with the little problems. They have demonstrated their skills. They know how to negotiate. They know how to sponge and mop. Now Linda must give them the supportive space to do it. Her strategy, creating "spill teams," creates a cooperative response to this daily occurrence, training children to stand in readiness much like volunteer firefighters to respond to sudden emergencies with calm precision and timely support. Solving the problem with spill teams is a concrete way of imbuing children with the confidence to fix a mistake and take on a responsibility. The spill teams move children from blame and accusation to reciprocity, what Piaget sees as central to moral understanding.

Linda's metaphor for her dilemma, "learning to let the spill grow," describes a familiar quandary for teachers. How long should we watch before we jump in and take over? We are afraid of losing control. What if the spill turns into a flood and gets far worse too fast? Literally we have seen children start to mop a small paint blot and suddenly the entire room is leaking, smearing soapy splatter. Not so literally, we have seen a small conflict between two children grow into a shouting, class-wide altercation. There are times when we should have stepped in earlier. As I argued previously, turning too much over to the children without proper instruction can lead to damaging outcomes. Giving children space to practice when they have been reasonably prepared seems a necessary risk. Children invested in cleaning up the spill are less likely to douse each other with paint or turn soapy towels into missiles. Children versed in a language of respect are less likely to hurl insults. That doesn't mean it will always work. We have bad days, off moods, and every year, Halloween.

Fear of sharing power may also deter us from letting the spill grow. That fear may grow as teachers move from a more traditional style of teaching to an approach that seeks more student participation and decision-making. As teachers, we must find our own momentum and our own pace of change. As our spill teams and problem solvers go to work, as we observe that these measures do work, we will begin to stand back and watch the spills with growing relief, biting lips perhaps while restraining the impulse to do the work for the children and at the same time gaining trust in our children and ourselves.

"I want children to be able to solve problems without always coming to the teacher," Linda writes. By spring, most of the first graders do solve problems without coming to their teacher first. However, the teacher is indeed present. Even when we don't see the teacher mopping up the spilled juice, we see the "teams" she helped put in place, we see the wonderful language she encouraged her children to learn, and we see the time and effort she has taken to help children move from blame to action, from anger to cooperation. We also see her recognition that some children need some extra doses of holding before they will be ready for more self-reliance. There are often, as we learn from this case, hidden or less visible needs that must be addressed if children are to be able to solve problems on their own. Language is a critical link. Here we see the power of naming, identifying the big and little problems.

Another important tool Linda has taught is listening. One of the children writes at the end of the year that he has learned "to really respect the person who is speaking." Sometimes children don't listen to each other. Teachers become the voice-over, telling them what the other has said, urging them to take heed. It appears that children's listening skills improve as they practice conversations and begin to act on spoken requests. Often we must begin by teaching children how to listen to their classmates.

I end this commentary by going back to the beginning. "Why did you select this problem?" I asked Linda in the fall when she had just started. The answer came not at the beginning but really at the end. The answer evolved from personal association, from her own experiences in school. Linda recalled that she had been a good pupil, pleasing and always obliging her teachers. In the process, she had somehow failed to learn something that she would come to value in terms of her own adult life—self-reliance. I too find that some of my strongest convictions and clear positives have grown out of my own experiences. Linda writes, "I want children to know what to do when conflicts arise. I want them to make choices that will be healthy for them." Many of us know that we had little guidance, certainly in school, to learn those skills, to come to see ourselves as capable of solving even little problems. We turned to our teachers, our parents, our more self-assured peers to do it for us. Self-reliance does not have to be achieved through defiance. It can be learned as we engage in our daily classroom routines. We can learn how to find a partner, ask for a place on the rug, clean up the spills and walk to the problem solving table, expecting our classmates to follow, ready to "Stop, Explain, Talk and Shake Hands."

CHAPTER SIX

OUTER STRUCTURES/
INNER SUPPORTS

Teaching Respect to Fourth and Fifth Graders

by Cathy Jacques

Cathy Jacques has been teaching elementary and middle school for seven years. Looking for "humanity and laughter," she returned to teaching after a 12-year absence and currently teaches at Community Preparatory School in Providence, Rhode Island. She holds a B.A. in elementary education from the University of Rhode Island.

When not teaching, Cathy pursues her interest in Celtic music and enjoys reading about medieval history. Her greatest pleasure comes from relaxing at home with her husband and two cats.

Classes had been dismissed for lunch and the hallway was alive with kids going into lockers, heading for rest rooms, and meeting friends. The principal had just stopped by the room to speak with me, and we were standing in the hall. Behind him I saw James and Patricia playfully arguing. Suddenly, with the grace of a dancer, Patricia's leg shot out and kicked a laughing James with a sideswipe worthy of Jean-Claude Van Damme.

"Patricia!" I brought my conversation with the principal to an abrupt halt.

"We were only fooling around, Ms. J." Patricia's smile faded; James's laughter turned into a silent frown.

"I don't care that you were only 'fooling around.' Play fighting is not allowed! This is exactly what we've been talking about so much lately! Keep your body to yourself!"

The stream of hungry children carried James and Patricia away, but not before I saw James give Patricia a sidelong glance, catch her eye, and smile . . . in triumph? My conversation with the principal resumed, but my attention was elsewhere. What had just happened?

A physical confrontation is rare at Community Prep; I can't say I've ever witnessed one during my years here. In fact, students often work hard to be respectful to each other in class. But physical "play" fighting, verbal intimidation, and name-calling, often disguised as "fun" and "play," occur often in the halls, the rest rooms, at recess and lunch. Students use these behaviors to test limits, establish peer groups, and develop hierarchies in what is for them a new environment.

When I came to Community Preparatory School, I wanted to include social skills as part of my classroom program. I had prior teaching experience in a Jewish day school where teaching "values" was a key part of the curriculum. Although religious parameters defined their program, I knew there was a place for addressing ethical and social skills within a secular framework.

We are an independent school, drawing a majority of our students from the poorest neighborhoods in the city of Providence. Economically and ethnically diverse, the school's student body consists of 110 to 120 students ranging from grades four through eight. We also have an inclusion program for some students at Rhode Island School for the Deaf. Theme-based curriculum, process-oriented teaching, community service learning, student-centered classrooms—clearly, the school has strong ingredients for a positive educational experience. Still, students seemed to lack a sense of personal responsibility.

During my first year here I had become increasingly convinced of the need to address social skills as I observed students yelling at one another, running down corridors, not allowing others to pass, letting doors slam shut in the face of the person walking behind, and exhibiting disruptive behaviors with seemingly no awareness of the effect on the other classes. My students were fine as long as they were under my supervision, but they exhibited unacceptable behaviors outside the classroom. As the fourth grade teacher, I also felt a responsibility to set the tone for the school academically and behaviorally; fourth grade, the entrance grade, needed to be the foundation for a successful experience at the school.

After a while I began routinely to complain about my students' and other students' behavior. Other faculty agreed that a problem existed, and we decided to proceed in small ways: monitoring hallways, discussing these issues in class and modeling appropriate behavior. Although needed and helpful, I felt these interventions were not enough, but I was fumbling for what to do. I tried a theme-based curricular approach to increase awareness of differences and similarities between classmates. We explored and celebrated our diversity and our commonality using theme topics to develop critical thinking skills about community, tolerance, and responsibility. The students responded thoughtfully, but the classroom power struggles persisted, students continued to use antagonistic language with each other, and few students showed common courtesies to others. I decided to provide more opportunities for my class to discuss specific issues.

Class discussion around social issues had been random so I began to have Class Meetings once a week. Every Wednesday morning for about one hour, students brought their concerns to the attention of the class, and everyone, in turn, discussed solutions. We might have concerns that certain students in the upper grades were teasing the fourth graders, lunch money was being stolen, or boys weren't treating girls equally at recess. Anything could be discussed, but two rules were established: everyone must listen and speak respectfully, and nothing that was said was to be discussed outside the classroom unless everyone agreed.

Our Class Meetings evolved further as the students chose to incorporate two distinct areas: 1) whole class announcements and problem-solving, and 2) "thoughts," a time when everyone shared a negative event in their life that made them feel sad or angry, followed by everyone sharing a positive, happy event. In the beginning of the year we only shared verbally, but later time was set aside for students to write response notes offering support or advice which they placed in their classmates' mailboxes. This opened the channels of communi-

cation even further. Students shared and listened to concerns involving class members as well as the wider school community.

On one occasion, a few kids brought up the fact that Warren was
distracting them a great deal in class. "Warren makes faces and weird
noises in science and won't do any work," said Danita. Others in the
class began nodding and agreeing with Danita's comment.

"Why does this upset you, Danita?" I asked.

"Because our group's not getting the project done, and I can't con-
centrate."

"Did you try talking to Warren about this?"

"I told him to get to work, but he won't listen to me!"

During this discussion, Warren crossed his arms, sat back in his
chair with his legs outstretched, and drew his eyebrows together. He
was offended, and his defensive body language let everyone know it.
A few others in the class gave similar stories, but two that surprised
Warren (and me) came from his close friends, Jamal and William.

"I go along with Warren a lot 'cause we're friends, but I don't like
it sometimes. I've been getting in trouble a lot lately," Jamal said, as
William nodded.

I asked Warren what he thought about what he heard. He
shrugged and looked upset, but refused any comments.

"It's pretty clear that a lot of kids in this class see this as a problem.
Do you?"

Warren finally broke his silence. "Yeah, but I can't help it."

"Well, that's OK. Let's see if we can figure out how to resolve this."

The class brainstormed ideas. After Warren explained he didn't
understand what his job was in the science group, Danita agreed to
help him get started. Others made an agreement with Warren that
when he began to get really distracting, they would tell him to help
him re-focus. Warren agreed to try. By the end of the meeting, there
was an action plan and a few smiles.

At the following week's Class Meeting, I asked for an update on
Warren's progress. He and his class felt things were better and the class
gave a round of applause for Warren's efforts. He and his classmates
continued to have difficulties, and we continued to tackle them, with
mixed results. It was significant to me, however, that the kids felt safe
and empowered to discuss problems, work together to find solutions,

and applaud individual and group efforts. Students began problem-solving on their own outside of the classroom and acquired the confidence to ask me to mediate their more personal concerns. This was a direct result of the climate and tone set by Class Meeting.

Over time, I could see some positive changes but I wondered if I had put too much emphasis on the big issues of respect, tolerance, and cooperation and not enough on *specific behaviors.* Raising student awareness, involving the whole school, modeling respect, and giving students opportunities to voice their concerns and applaud other students'

efforts were all important but we also needed to teach specific behaviors. I worked with the other teachers in my team to develop an outline of specific social skills that we would teach and discuss with our fourth and fifth graders.

These measures, along with improved discipline in the school (immediate and direct intervention as issues arose; more structure overall) and the continuation and expansion of Class Meetings, resulted in noticeable improvement in the school climate. Students were helping other students more; "hello," "please" and "thank you" were heard more often and there appeared to be fewer in-class distractions.

As we entered into the last quarter of the year, however, there was a decline in the use of the social skills we'd taught, and an increase in inappropriate behavior—physical contact, abusive language, name-calling, lack of concern for personal, school, and other people's property. Although communication remained open, I couldn't understand why, after seven months of meetings and discussions about behavior, students were unable or unwilling to apply the skills they had been taught when they were away from supervised settings.

I thought back to a conversation we had in September. I had asked my fourth grade class, "What is a leader?" They had compiled a fine list of leadership attributes including "honesty," "being fair," "a good listener," "encourages others." My next question was, "What is a friend?" They offered a few of the same characteristics, but the single most important item on this list was "fun."

"I want a friend who's fun to play with."

"She has to have a good sense of humor."

"Fun" and "playful" can be positive qualities that children use to test and practice behaviors they will use as adults. The negative side of this idea of fun came up during a Class Meeting where the issue of name-calling arose. Class Meeting is a time set aside for talking about class concerns, so I asked the class why calling names was a concern, and why they thought this was happening. Jack answered defensively, "We don't mean anything. We're just playing around; we're friends."

When I asked them if there was any difference between "play fighting" and "name-calling," Kevin said, "If you play fight, you can get hurt."

"So, are you saying you can't hurt anyone when you call them names?"

"Well, yeah, but . . . not really."

"Yes, you can," said Nicholas. "Some kids won't stop even if you ask them to."

The conversation was short, and although Jack reluctantly agreed that name-calling was inappropriate, the smile he shared with some others in the class showed he didn't sincerely believe it. Importantly though, some children like Nicholas, who had been hurt by name-calling, had spoken out.

I wanted my students to have the internal supports to sustain the positive behaviors we were working on in the classroom. It was clear that the problem would not be solved solely through imposed structure. In thinking about this case study, I asked myself, "What do I need to do to help these kids develop more self-control and exercise better judgment away from adult supervision?" I decided that I needed to *observe* more, *ask* more questions, and—with the students—*determine a course of action.*

As I *observed*, I discovered that many of the behaviors that troubled me were between friends: physical expressions like bumping and kicking; name-calling ("Hey, butt-head, sit over here!"). I also *observed* that it was nearly always punctuated by laughter from the people on the giving and receiving end.

I called a fourth grade Class Meeting and asked whether anyone saw any behavior that they would consider to be a problem. A few kids said, "Not really," and others shrugged or looked blankly at me. I mentioned, in general, what I had been seeing.

"It's not just us. The eighth graders have been mean to us, too."

"Yeah, the fifth grade, too."

"The sixth grade is okay though."

I acknowledged that the behavior seemed to be almost school-wide, but I did not let them use that as an excuse. Instead I pursued the problem with them. I asked, "What does it feel like when kids use name-calling or bossy behavior?" I got the following exchange:

Freddy: "It feels bad, Ms. J."

Andrew: "It depends. It can be funny, but when *you* get upset, it's not funny anymore."

Gerald: "It was funny at first, but then it hurt my feelings and she wouldn't stop when I asked her to."

Charles: "It's exciting."

I was struck by Charles's statement. "Why do you say that, Charles?" After some thought, he said, "You don't know what's gonna happen next."

Charles was talking about the same "excitement" that keeps kids reading *Goosebumps* books. Tension and suspense are alluring. Many young children are unable or unwilling to distinguish between the excitement that derives from positive tension and that which comes from negative tension. I realized that I needed to help them distinguish between these different types of excitement and help them recognize consequences that can result from each type. We talked more about why some behaviors are negative, but when our discussion ended I still felt troubled by Charles's statement. How can respectful behavior compete when it is perceived as slow and dull, and disrespect has such immediacy and power?

Then, just as these class discussions seemed to be leading somewhere positive, we had to take a one month break so my student teacher could have more time to work on a special social studies project with the class. When we finally returned to holding Class Meetings, students eagerly shared their pent-up thoughts, and I felt connected to them again. The break was necessary to accommodate the scope of the projects, but the month off had been stressful. More than anything else, this break clarified the relationship between some of our class rituals and student behavior. In the presence of stress, internal controls weaken and inappropriate behavior increases. Everyone needs constructive, positive outlets for emotional and physical tension. When the class was under a lot of academic pressure with few opportunities to share feelings, the value of Class Meetings as a ritualized pressure-reliever became clear.

PETER WRENN

As a final writing assignment, I asked my class to brainstorm problems in the school that concerned them. They produced a long list and included such topics as bragging, disrespect for others' property, and cliques. I then asked everyone to choose one to write about. By far, the one chosen most was name-calling. I explained my involvement with this case study project, and described the process of focusing on a problem, *observing, questioning,* and *determining a course of action.* I asked my students to follow the same process when planning and writing their essays.

The class as a whole began discussing their "problems." A few worked hard at following the process, observing behavior, and interviewing students. One student, Monica Rodriguez, wrote:

> I believe name-calling is a major problem of today. It hurts and it makes people feel unsafe. Name-calling should stop!
>
> I once talked with a girl who was often name-called. You would be surprised to hear what she said. She told me it hurts more if a friend is name-calling, but is just playing, than if a normal person is telling you off. She understood her friends didn't mean to hurt her, but yet they did. They put her down. For example, one day I saw Debra laughing hysterically. I went over to her and asked her what was so funny. She said, "You should have seen Tracy's laugh! She laughed like a witch!" Near her was Anthony also laughing at Tracy. There was Tracy, fighting back tears, for Debra was a close friend. You see how Tracy was embarrassed and was put down for her individuality?
>
> Another type of name-calling is when people are arguing. For example, one afternoon Jack called me a bunch of names based on my name, culture, language, looks, and family. Now Jack had offended me badly. I broke out into tears, for I could not hold it back. He had taken a piece out of me in a way. He put me down for who I was. Playing or not, I felt like punching Jack and name-calling him back. But I held it back, for I knew my name-calling him and fighting him would do no good. It would only get me in trouble and make me a bad person.
>
> You see, name-calling gets you nowhere. It only makes you a bad person and somebody nobody wants to hang out with. You should use all your energy for good things, not bad!

All the students read their essays to the class. I was astounded afterwards when Jack told me he would no longer "name-call." I gave him a doubtful look, skeptical that such a transformation could take place so quickly, but Jack didn't bow to my skepticism. He looked at me and said, "No, really, Ms. J. I didn't know it hurt so many people." Jack had really listened to Monica. I was touched by how her words had affected him. Not everyone responded in the same way, but Jack's reaction to Monica gave me hope.

This project has caused many questions to surface and resurface. I began by struggling with the problem of children following different behavior rules depending on whether they were inside class or beyond the classroom walls. Discussions with the children have convinced me that first I will need to confront the satisfaction they derive from negative behavior. This then will be my next struggle—how to help respectful behavior compete with negative excitement. I know now that children need internal supports to sustain their positive behavior, particularly in the face of pressure or stress. As I watched behavior deteriorate in the absence of Class Meetings, I became convinced that children need regular opportunities to talk about their feelings and listen to each other. By structuring conversations and building them into a regular schedule, we give children an outlet for relief during those inevitable times when internal supports collapse. Perhaps respectful behavior can begin to compete with negative excitement when enough structures provide positive, fun outlets for emotional and physical tension.

My case study is far from finished. My observations and conversations with my class have raised many questions that I hope to pursue next year. What constructive ways can teachers give children to have thrills, excitement, and positive fun in school? How can we help children distinguish between negative and positive tension so they can begin to choose wisely when the teacher is not around? How can we help

> I became convinced that children need regular opportunities to talk about their feelings and listen to each other. By structuring conversations and building them into a regular schedule, we give children an outlet for relief during those inevitable times when internal supports collapse.

young children tease apart the threads so they know when something is exciting for positive reasons rather than exciting because it's hurtful? This will be my next step as I struggle to help children find pleasure in supporting each other rather than in playfully hurting each other. It is difficult to end a year with so many questions. Still, when I think about how much Jack learned from listening to Monica, I become excited to think I might finally be beginning to grapple with a piece of behavior that has bothered me for a long time.

RUTH'S COMMENTARY *Outer Structures/Inner Supports*

Cathy Jacques initiated her case study in the spring. The emphasis and focus during this shorter time frame helps us see how a problem takes shape. Her primary interventions enable both teacher and students to identify and name the issues they are confronting. It is a very worthwhile and revealing process.

The narrative begins with an incident that will be highly familiar to all teachers, regardless of the grade taught. Two children are fooling around. With great innocence they even protest when rebuked by their teacher, "We were only fooling around." To the reader, this event might also seem too playful, too petty to bother about. This is not a serious fight or abridgment of the rules. Why fix on this one? Why does a busy teacher have to take time out to even speak about it, let alone worry about it or write a case study from it? Yet it is just such an incident which signals the start of social interactions which so often go awry. Cathy Jacques reminds us that this type of behavior has become so entrenched in the social conventions of our children that adults are coming to accept it without careful scrutiny.

The case grows out of frustration and a question. What is this behavior and why is it so persistent particularly once children are out of the classroom? Her concern evolves from dealing with an irritating moment to examining a more complex and entrenched social issue. Over the course of the case study we see it gather definition and clarity. By the end of the case, conversations between teacher and students develop more mutual understanding of divergent perceptions. Observation and dialogue animate and drive this exchange, adding not to ready solutions but to a better understanding of the nature of the problem. Even for the students, the problem entails more than the messiness of getting caught. They confront some of the messy implications of "play fighting."

Cathy Jacques' initial observation of Patricia and James compels her attention. Through the weekly structured ritual of Class Meetings, the students begin to discuss play fighting in its different ramifications. "What's the difference between name-calling and play fighting?" the teacher asks. Some students see a connection. Others do not. Gradually two different views of play fighting emerge. One equates much of play fighting with name-calling, and name-calling is generally agreed to be spiced with hurtful insults. The second view of play fighting, named by Charles but clearly acknowledged in the smiles of the first incident, is that it's exciting. "You don't know what's going to happen," Charles replies when asked what he means by exciting. There are often elements of tension and the unknown even in the most circumscribed children's play: who will win, who will step on the rope, who will land on free parking, who will grab the chair when the music stops? As the children talk about play fighting, it is clear that the elements of risk are high. Will someone get upset, mad, laugh, win? Making fun is clearly an important need for these children and for all children. Cathy worries that, in fact, respectful behavior is seen by kids as too dull and slow to ever compete with the power of disrespect.

As her class looks closer at this problem which has the potential to excite and to hurt, we see the teacher and the students evidence puzzlement and doubt. Even as the answers seem less than obvious, the teacher continues to use her Class Meetings to ask questions and listen to responses. In June, we read the journal entry of a fifth grader who writes about name-calling, "It hurts and it makes people feel unsafe. Name-calling should stop." We even see that Jack is affected by what he hears. While his teacher is less convinced by his promise to stop, he seems to say truthfully that he didn't know what he did "hurt so many people."

Do we believe that? I tend to find that children do not generally realize their ability both to hurt and to support each other. They do not often see themselves as effective and important. So many of their attempts to gain status or attention end up as false. They pose, they hustle, they dramatize and they act cool. This prevents them from seeing their enormous potential to fix things, to act on the things that matter most to them in the world. Their actions seem to be caught in a perpetual limbo between passivity and aggression, leaving them unable to exert their real strengths. So I am not sure whether they truly do know how hurtful they can be. Even when they are hurt by someone else's insults, that may not generalize to "if I get hurt , others will, too." I also do not see children who are sufficiently aware of their positive capacities. I once mentioned to my own class of eighth graders that it bothered me that so few of them had made an effort to say hello and ask me how I felt after being home sick for a week. I got back a sheepish look from some, but confusion from others. It never occurred to them that this adult teacher might need or want something from them. We often don't share with our students their critical role in fixing things and accomplishing hard tasks. We do not invite them into the struggle. In this powerful process of Class Meetings, fourth graders begin to define and confront an aspect of their social life. Initial resistance gives way to shared ownership and interest.

In another discussion, students confront a particular classmate. Their accusations are specific and pointed. Warren, who is the target, listens even as his friends join in. As I read this account, I can feel both the justification of the complaints and Warren's unease. I see this as a good example of how teachers can give students an important role without unchecked license. Cathy allows a direct conversation, but she insists on a positive outcome. Warren, however annoying and disruptive, must not be shunned. Respectful exchange is an assumption of the Class Meeting structure. The children take this task seriously. Even their complaints are voiced as specific behaviors (faces, weird noises, not working) rather than as attacks on Warren. The discussion ends with a proposal to help him focus and understand his work, and Warren agrees to try. It is important to note that Warren does acknowledge the problem. The class also gives him input on finding positive and productive strategies. Success is judged by the teacher not so much on the basis of the mixed results of the student's progress, but the growing safety of the class to work on these problems. It seems to me a real accomplishment that these children are learning to "applaud individual and group efforts." As they develop these tools, Cathy finds that they are acquiring the confidence to problem-solve more outside their room and to mediate (not fight) over more personal concerns.

I pointed out in Eileen Mariani's case that when children lack social skills, we often eliminate social opportunities. An alternative is to provide structures which help children develop their social skills. The Class Meeting ritual used in this class is a structure that promotes social skills. It gives children a place to learn to speak respectfully even about personal and difficult issues. Cathy's Class Meetings require that children listen to each other. As the children develop the habit of active listening (keeping their hands down when others are speaking, keeping their eyes on the speaker, giving responses related to the speaker's remarks), they begin to hear and acknowledge different perspectives, laying a foundation for empathy. In these class meetings children begin to understand the results of their actions toward one another—to see their ability to make others feel good or bad. The way that Cathy Jacques guides these discussions permits honest opinions but also requires that empathy be a strong part of the invention of practical strategies. Cathy uses Class Meetings as a ritual to help students reach towards their "best selves" and act on that potential. In the discussions about play fighting and Warren, we see that the practice of listening to each other bears results. Jack hears that name-calling may hurt. Warren hears that his antics bother even his friends. Piaget wrote that "respect is the source of moral obligation." He said further that cooperation helps children understand intentionality "by forcing the individual to be constantly occupied with the point of view of other people so as to compare it with their own." (Piaget, 1965, p. 190) I find that as children see this intentionality, they are better able to enter into a discussion of alternatives. We need to help children see the power and excitement that mutual respect creates. In fact, mutual respect makes Class Meetings possible.

Recently, I had the opportunity to visit Community Prep and to see many of Cathy's students in a Class Meeting in their present classroom. Not surprisingly the first agenda item initiated by three of the girls was about name-calling. "Everybody is crackin' during lunch." There were twenty large bodies in the circle and two visitors. Everyone was sitting up, bodies almost leaning into the topic. The discussion that followed was stunning in its articulation, honest illustrations, controversy and discipline. Not once did the teacher have to call people to order or attend to rude or off-task behavior. Yet there were intense feelings voiced. The only disciplinary measure came from another student who pointed out that it was annoying when people raised their hands while others were talking. "I do it too," he added, "but I wish people could just keep their hands down." And then moments later I watched as this same student gave a speedy little signal to a classmate who had forgotten. Zip—her hand went down.

The students agreed that the name-calling snowballed. They agreed that it was often about things you couldn't control like appearance. And one young woman added, "You should be able to come to school the way you are and be respected." Such poetry and wisdom from a twelve year old and said with such a serious tone! There was more disagreement about what to do about the problem. Someone said, "Tell the teacher." Someone else said that there needed to be more dire consequences. Another student said that consequences wouldn't do anything "because once you start it's never ever over." "Ignore, make a joke (not an insult), tell the teacher" were suggested but none seemed to gain strong appeal. Then the teacher and I did a "role play" to show what happens and to make the problem more concrete. I went after his shoes. He came back. I went after his pin (a more touchy possession). He went after my face. By that time the class was well into our theatrical performance. They laughed, cheered, hooted and clapped. We had our audience. At that point we stopped and asked the question, "What just happened?" They observed with utter accuracy. They saw that it got bad fast, from shoes (which one student pointed out you can change) to a face (which you can't). They also saw their own role in the exchange—how they had encouraged and urged and made it harder for one of us to back down. We wanted the children to begin to see that sometimes a situation includes more than the individuals immediately involved, and that perhaps they needed to find a new way to have fun. In any case, the solution wasn't found that day. Questions were raised. "Can we put it on the agenda for next week?" "Can we do more role plays?"

Again, I was struck by the respectful attention of all the students in this circle. Their discussion was never dull or slow, and there were no insults or put-downs (even facial ones). It may not yet transfer into lunchroom social time, but they showed another way to interact and they were inspiring.

Is this observation relevant to Cathy's case study? I think so. Both the outer structure and the inner supports have continued. The children are still struggling with the issue of play fighting. It is still full of mixed messages. The continuity of the Class Meeting ritual demonstrates ongoing commitment and interest. I felt the students were deeply invested in the particular problem and in the use of the Class Meeting itself. It also struck me that these children were trying to build a community out of the deep divisions that mark society today. Community Prep is interracial, with children of color in the majority. It is also economically mixed. Many students come from inner city, welfare families, some from working poor and a smaller number from privileged homes. Around this circle of students it was possible to see and to hope that diversity and harmony can coexist.

Finally, Cathy's case also identifies that other aspect of play fighting—the excitement. This revelation occurs just as the year is ending, leaving us with resonating questions. One question asked is what are the ways that school structures time for fun? How do we help children vent, relax, release their sizable physical and emotional energies? Are there ways to channel and structure that need for excitement into constructive play? I am reminded again of Geoffrey Canada's (1995) warning that when adults do not provide for children's basic needs they devise their own ways which are often not acceptable. When we ignore the need for play, it goes underground. Fun, according to psychologist William Glasser, is fundamental for personal and community well-being. (Glasser, 1990) We do know that laughter wards off illness, diminishes stress and prepares us to go back to work. I have heard teachers worry that if they let kids have fun, they won't get them back. But I find the opposite to be true. When we let them have fun, they want to come back.

It is a risk to share questions with our students which we cannot answer. Even if they all wanted to stop "play fighting" (and they don't), even if they wanted to tease only in funny ways, the lines between insult and humor have become so blurred that we can never ensure that the "fun" will be completely harmless. Yet out of this difficult issue, we see the elements of social growth. Children are entering into respectful dialogue; they are taking interest and learning from one another. They are seeing the connections between what they say and what they do.

Questions and structures first raised in fourth grade are practiced and used again in fifth and now in sixth. Given this opportunity, we also begin to see inner growth—in the student who reminds others to keep their hands down, the beautiful wish that all could come as they are and be respected, the brave voice of Monica that says "name-calling gets you nowhere" and Jack's promise to try to stop name-calling, a triumph of active listening. From this case, it seems clear that the teacher's voice is best used not to lecture but to provide those powerful structures that give her children a voice and a way to really listen to one another.

It seems to me that children, particularly those in that awkward phase of adolescence, are crying out for respect. In this community the slang code word for disrespect was "crackin'." I have also heard it called dissing, ranking, sounding, one-upmanship and hazing. It is not a new phenomenon. Has it reached more epidemic proportions? Or are we more frightened by it now because when teasing erupts into violence, the disputes are fought with lethal weapons? We have reason to be afraid for our children and we have reason to intervene and help them before violence snowballs. The interventions I see in Cathy Jacques' study show me an alternative and, most importantly, they show the children alternatives. We might order silence in the lunchroom, employ the National Guard to monitor the conversations, or as Cathy shows us, we can implement structures that teach social skills. Children will not learn them overnight, but with the persistence and regularity of our best curriculum, they will treat each other differently.

"Mr. Connor," I said as I was leaving his classroom, "I really do like your shoes." Mr. Connor laughed.

"Mr. Connor," a student interjected, a graduate of Cathy's class, "Now you're supposed to say you like her face!"

Chapter Seven

HOW ARE YOU GOING TO UNBORE YOURSELF?

Active Learning in the Fifth Grade

by Colette Kaplan

Colette Funteral Kaplan has been teaching for twenty-one years and loves it! She has had many diversified teaching experiences ranging from teaching kindergarten to grade eight in both private and public schools, in rural and urban communities. She especially enjoyed teaching children of migrant workers.

Colette completed her undergraduate studies at Eastern Connecticut State University and completed her master's degree at the University of Connecticut.

Colette enjoys traveling with her two children, Dana and Joshua. She also enjoys reading both adult and children's literature. She enjoys dining out—but doesn't like to cook.

Pagels School is a K–6 school with 380 students in the city of West Haven, Connecticut. Most of the children come right from the neighborhood which is a very stable community. Many of my 27 fifth graders this year have been in school together since kindergarten. By now, they know each other's strengths and weaknesses and generally relate well to one another.

My choice of a topic to study in this project was prompted by an incident in my classroom that upset me. From this "upsetting" incident came a year of growth for the students and me.

It's so Boring!

It was an October day, early in the week, and my energy was high. I was particularly looking forward to our social studies period, eager to watch my fifth graders dig into their projects on Native Americans. I had worked hard to structure the unit in a way that gave students lots of opportunity for choice while still insuring that they mastered information I believe is important to their understanding of American history. The preparation I had done for this unit fascinated me and I was pleased to note my students' excitement during the first few days of this study.

Anna and Claudia had chosen to work together studying Native American dwellings. This morning found them sitting at a cluster of desks, chatting quietly. Their desktops were empty—no papers, no books, no art supplies. I stationed myself nearby, but chose not to intervene yet. I pushed down the irritation that I felt as the minutes ticked by and they showed no sign of activity. Perhaps they were planning their work together. My eavesdropping soon shattered this hope. Their talk had nothing to do with longhouses or teepees; it concerned the morning's recess.

"I'm so sick of kickball," grumbled Claudia.

"I know," agreed Anna. "We never do anything fun."

"Yeah, it's so boring."

I felt my irritation surging. A gorgeous fall morning like this with twenty-five classmates to play with, a chance to choose whatever game they wanted, and they're *bored?* ranted my inner voice. I myself had spent so much time getting ready for the day's activities that I had little sympathy for their complaint.

When their conversation lagged, they seemed content to sit quietly. Anna's long arm stretched across an adjacent chair, her head resting on it, her eyes tracking the progress of a noisy fly circling the room. Claudia was even less animated. Elbows on her desk, she cupped her chin in her hands, her eyes unmoving as she stared into space.

I couldn't stand it any longer. I pulled a chair up next to them and waited for them to turn toward me. "Are you girls having difficulty getting started today?" They exchanged nervous glances; they had been "caught!" Anna bent down and fiddled with her shoelace, leaving Claudia to save them.

"We're bored," she announced.

Anna's head popped up at that point. "Yeah," she chimed in helpfully, "We have nothing to do. We finished the teepee and now we have nothing to do and it's boring."

That word again! Boring.

I took a deep breath and worked to keep a strident tone out of my voice. "Tell me about the part you finished and let's figure out where you might go next." With my help they decided that they needed to make a sign for the teepee and begin modeling a longhouse out of clay. They got to work and used the remaining fifteen minutes well.

I See the Problem

On my way home late that afternoon, my thoughts drifted back to the classroom. *We're bored . . . bored . . . bored.* My head had turned into an echo chamber, and I felt irritation again. In fact, what I felt, if I looked inward honestly, went beyond irritation. It was anger.

I lectured myself. "What's going on here? It wasn't such a big deal. A couple of girls who are basically fine students wasted half a period. You intervened and they got back to work. A teacher's day is full of directions and re-directions. Why are you so aggravated?"

"But, it isn't just Claudia and Anna." The conversation I'd overheard and the one I'd been directly involved in were variations on a theme that repeated all too often in this fifth grade. Sometimes it manifested as a sigh, a rolling of eyes; sometimes students simply sat passively while around them the room buzzed with activity.

In my classroom I expect all students to participate, share, cooperate, respect, and do their best. It frustrated me to hear "I'm bored" or to observe the body language of boredom. I want students to be actively engaged in their learning, to inform me of their interests, to expand on what is happening in the classroom.

I thought back to my own elementary school years. I was a good student, and school was generally easy for me, but I never had the opportunity to expand on any area of interest. I was never asked to delve into any topic with passion. I passively answered the questions at the end of each chapter in the social studies book, read the science chapters, wrote on assigned topics. Always at the assigned pace, always in the assigned mode. I quickly memorized the dates and names required for the tests, and I quickly forgot them afterwards! I walked quite competently through my assigned education.

I don't want my students to "walk through" an education I assign. To me, this means stopping to investigate topics of interest. It means being given opportunity to focus on a small segment of a topic to learn some new facts or gain insight. I want to give children an allowance—allow them time to imagine, to expand, and to grow. For this to happen they have to become invested in their education. They must want to have a say in what they learn and how they learn. It won't happen if they're bored.

As I reflected, I realized that I had happened upon issues I cared very deeply about. It wasn't that I simply wanted to ban all forms of the word "bore" from Room 27. (Though that might be a fine and satisfying thing!) I wanted students to participate in their learning, to really become actively involved in learning. I wanted them to recognize their own boredom and passivity, to become uncomfortable with it, and develop some strategies for changing it. I didn't want them simply to offer it up to me to solve, much as Claudia and Anna had today.

I began to feel my irritation melting, shifting shape, and emerging as excitement. I now saw the specific incident of the day as part of a bigger pattern. I had identified a problem I was really interested in tackling, and I felt a resolution taking shape: by the end of this year, I would understand more about this beast named Boredom and about teaching fifth graders how to conquer it.

I Take Time to Observe

Many times I had resolved to spend more time observing my own classroom, but it was never an easy resolution to carry out. There were so many tasks always calling out to me, and so many students who could benefit from a few minutes of my attention. Observing always fell to the bottom of my to-do list. Having this assignment moved it to the top, and in November I consciously observed students at least once a day!

Those observations revealed to me that some of the "I'm bored" responses occurred when a child or group was "done." They said "I'm done; I have nothing to do; I'm bored." When I looked at their work I usually saw that they had not taken enough time or put much effort into their project or assignment.

Another observation sent my thoughts in a different direction, and made me realize that "boring" was a catchall word that meant a lot of different things. It was math class, and I was focusing my observation upon Samantha. Samantha often makes sarcastic remarks, and frequently comments, "I hate math. It's boring."

This period began with those same old remarks which I dutifully recorded on my legal pad. Several students near her were working together on the division problem I had assigned and automatically turned to her to include her in their wonderings. Jenny leaned eagerly across the table to peer at Samantha's paper.

"Let's see how you did that!" she exclaimed, grabbing Samantha's paper and tilting it so that she could read what was on it.

Samantha grabbed it back. "Like you can't figure it out yourself!" she retorted, crumpling her paper in her hand and folding her arms across her chest.

I glanced at my watch. Fifteen out of the twenty minutes I had promised myself to observe had gone by. Close enough. I couldn't bear to watch and let this situation build.

I called Samantha aside and sat down with her. Pushing past her sarcasm and exaggerated sighs, I wrote out a few problems, simpler than the one I had given the class, and calmly said, "Forget the other assignment. Get to work on these."

Samantha sighed loudly, shifted in her seat, and rolled her eyes to make sure I understood that she was not happy. I braced myself for the expected refrain. Sure enough: "I think math's boring, you know." Yes, she had let me know that, I assured her. "I want to see you do this anyway," I stated firmly and she got to work. I watched her struggle with the two-digit multiplication problem I had composed, erasing so often that she wore a hole in her paper.

It was obvious that she had difficulty with the procedure, though I knew that her grasp of basic number facts was strong. As I talked through the problem with her, I realized that she had hidden her difficulty by her interruptions, her sarcasm, and her bored posture. On that day she acknowledged that she has trouble remembering the order of certain math procedures. I told her that I had helped many students who had very similar problems, and that I was sure I could help her. We set up a time to meet and go over some strategies before the period ended.

It seemed so obvious as I looked back on that incident. I couldn't believe that I hadn't spotted what was going on before that day. I think that it would have taken me even longer, had it not been for the observer's stance I forced myself to take. Somehow giving myself permission not to have to react immediately, to really note all the words and nuances of the situation, gave me a clearer perspective. Samantha showed me the necessity of digging beneath the surface of "boring."

I SEARCH FOR MY CLEAR POSITIVE

December arrived with its bustle of holiday activities and an early onslaught of icy weather. Several snow days interrupted the school routine and my schedule of observing. The Christmas vacation provided me with some welcome time to reflect and re-focus.

At some point I had begun to wonder if I had selected a really worthy problem. Was this issue one that all good teachers had solved long ago? I knew I was learning a great deal from watching my students, but I wasn't entirely sure where to go next.

Then I received a letter from Ruth in which she summarized what she had gathered from my study so far. She related a similar incident that had happened in her own classroom recently, and I felt reassured that even someone I regarded as such a skilled teacher still struggled with this same problem. She posed some further questions that I might consider and offered several ideas. Among them was the suggestion that I articulate my Clear Positive and then bring it to the students as part of a discussion with them about what the word "boring" means.

I take my job very seriously and believe in providing a year filled with academics, opportunities to expand an interest and develop new skills, and time to have fun. But I have learned that I should not and will not be an entertainer. I will not take responsibility for seeing that all children are entertained and *not* bored.

Over this vacation I thought about Ruth's suggestions, and I also had an interesting conversation with my friend and colleague Linda Mathews. Although Linda teaches younger children, I always find talking with her helpful. I think she is masterful at finding the right questions to open conversations with children, and I mulled over her and Ruth's words as I planned for a discussion with my students.

I worked to articulate my Clear Positive. We will not be bored in this class. No, didn't work. Sounded like some chant from *The Wizard of Oz* in my ears. And besides, that might just imply that I had to be a better entertainer. And that was far from what I intended. I take my job very seriously and believe in providing a year filled with academics, opportunities to expand an interest and develop new skills, and time to have fun. But I have learned that I should not and will not be an entertainer. I will not take responsibility for seeing that all children are entertained and *not* bored. That must be up to them. I'll give them every opportunity to work on something and I'll encourage their endeavors. I'll praise, applaud, guide, and teach, but I won't take away responsibility for learning and engaging.

I realized that my thought process had led me to my Clear Positive for my students: *I want school this year to be a place where we are all active, involved learners. I don't want you to be bored. But I won't unbore you. My goal is for you to be able to do that for yourself.*

WHAT DOES BORING MEAN? THE DISCUSSION

We all returned in January ready to get back to work. The students remembered how choppy December's few school weeks had felt and even said that they hoped there wouldn't be any snow days for a while! It seemed a great time for The Discussion.

The next morning, on the Morning Message chart which I prepare and which students read as they enter the room, I asked them to think about what "boring" means. When we met, I went around the circle and students offered their definitions. I kept a list on the chart as we went around.

Everyone was given an opportunity to respond, saying "Pass" if they chose. Only three children passed, and when offered a second chance, they too responded. At the end, the list looked something like this.

"Boring" means
nothing to do
when I'm annoyed
done that before

confused
waiting
running out of ideas
don't want to
time reasons—not enough time to do what you want to or too
     much time available

Some students stated that boring was usually centered around math.
At their suggestion, I made a subtopic on the chart.

Math
too hard
can't get it
already know it
too easy
rushing

I made a mental note to myself to take a good look at my math
program and the way I'd configured it, but I really wanted to keep a
broader focus for the discussion. They continued for perhaps another
20–30 minutes and everyone was engaged and involved. There didn't
seem to be any bored students here!

"Paul. You've been waiting patiently to say something for the last
few minutes."

"Well, I was just wondering," he ventured, "how about when it's
snack time and the teacher keeps the class talking and talking, and
thinking and thinking, and you're really hungry and you wouldn't
mind moving? Could that be boring, too?"

OK, I got the message. End of discussion for today.

THE GRAPEVINE BOX AND THE BORING BOOK

The next day I reopened the discussion by telling the students how
thought-provoking I had found their definitions about boredom. A few
students had further thoughts about what kept people from getting excited or interested, and after they shared them, I turned the chart paper
to the next page where I had carefully written out my Clear Positive.

We read it together, and they seemed quite caught by the word
"unbore." Was it a real word, they wondered?

"It is in this room!" I proclaimed.

I let them know that we would be working on learning to unbore ourselves in a number of ways. Throughout these winter months we used many of our already established classroom structures to focus upon the issue. We often held Class Meetings, for example, to problem-solve together, and we now used some of those times to suggest techniques when a member of a cooperative team was having difficulty getting started, didn't feel like participating, said they were bored with the project.

We also already had in place something called The Grapevine. When students saw something positive happen, they jotted it down and inserted it in the Grapevine Box. Once a week the box was emptied and the contents were read aloud. I asked students to try extra hard to notice instances when others were interested, engaged, unbored, and to add those to the box.

And we began a Class Book to which each student would eventually contribute a page. Each page defined "boring means . . ." and then dealt with how to unbore yourself in such a situation. "Boring means . . ." came easily to most students, but unboring yourself was certainly challenging. At first students seemed uninvested in these pages, but as we talked about the book together we began to see it as a valuable resource that could be consulted by any of us and even by future classes. It would remind us to pause and think before resigning ourselves to boredom. Acknowledging that this book would serve a real purpose, that it was not just writing for the teacher, was a definite motivator.

LINCOLNLAND

And then a really pivotal thing happened. We had been studying Abraham Lincoln and I was looking for a way to harness some of the midwinter energy buildup that was hovering in the air. I hit upon the idea of a whole-class project; we would build a log cabin from empty carpet rolls which I begged from a local warehouse. Another teacher and I designed the basic construction, but students were in charge of the details and the actual construction. What a monumental project! We spent days researching log cabins. Students found pictures, computer printouts, books which dealt with log cabins and specifically Lincoln's log cabin.

After a week of investigation, small groups made models using different plans. During several days of construction I noticed only rare moments when children were not involved, usually because they needed more materials, or had run up against a design problem they needed help solving. At one point a group of girls became frustrated by their inability to glue paper towel rolls together for their model. The rolls kept rolling and the log cabin kept falling apart before they could secure it. By the end of three or four attempts the girls were ready to quit. Hearing them describe their problem to me, Tony came over to demonstrate his method of notching the ends of the rolls. They then joined forces with him and all worked on a combined model. Another slight glitch developed when I discovered Jeffrey had not chosen to be involved in any of the projects. The projects didn't look like fun, he explained. A private conversation revealed that he wanted to saw the logs, but was afraid to admit that he didn't know how to use the saw.

I explained that none of us knew how to saw carpet rolls. We were all just learning and training each other and he needed to pick a job that he wanted to learn to do. In the end he chose sawing, joined right in, and became involved and interested.

Our project took approximately five to six weeks from conception to completion. It culminated with a "Lincolnland Tour" which we conducted for all the students in our school. The Tour included all the papers and projects which emerged from the investigation period, a video of the making of the cabin, and a mini-play of Lincoln's life. The day of the Tour was exhausting for all the fifth graders, acting as docents in our museum and talking and explaining all day.

At day's end we all stood back and admired our log cabin. It measured 10.5 feet by 8 feet and was 7 feet high. We giggled, laughed and congratulated ourselves. We shared what we saw as our greatest accomplishments. Every single student felt pride. Even Kevin, a real holdout on the Boring Front, agreed that he had had fun and had enjoyed telling other Pagels students about the cabin. I loved it when he reported indignantly, "Do you know that some kids talked when *we* talked? And *some* kids didn't pay attention!"

After two weeks, I was informed that our log cabin had to come down. Apparently its carpet roll and newspaper construction made it a fire hazard. When I told the class this, their faces fell. They grumbled and complained throughout the morning until I decided they needed a forum and convened the class. I questioned the kids: "Why do you think taking the cabin down bothers you so much? We knew that it could only stand for a short while."

The hands shot up. They had very definite ideas about why they were bothered.

"It took a long time to build."

"We want to go in it to read and work."

"We worked hard!"

Emphatic noises and nods of agreement followed this last comment.

I pushed further: "And why does it bother you to take down something that you obviously worked hard on?"

"We hate to lose all that work."

"I want to see it for a while longer."

"We are proud of what we built."

More nods of agreement all around.

The Log Cabin Standard

This discussion—the project, in fact—became a reference point to which we returned over and over during the remainder of the year as we continued to develop strategies for unboring ourselves. It had provided us with a common experience, a time when we all felt the pleasure that immersion in work we are proud of can bring. We compared this project with more mundane assignments. We came to realize that not all work holds this much interest; not all work is hands-on construction work; some work is by nature more mundane and tedious. The log cabin became a standard by which we could measure our "unboredom," our involvement. *What do you notice about this writing assignment? How do you feel about your final product? Do you feel the sense of achievement you felt with the log cabin? Why? Why not?*

The Challenge of Critiquing

Although by mid-April I noticed real growth in students' ability to examine their own and each other's work, it was difficult for me to try to find the proper way to teach children how to critique their work. At meeting, we often looked at a piece of work, studying it closely. The students were eager to note the details. They often commented, "I like what you've done," but it was still a challenge to get them beyond that. When I questioned a student about his piece, I frequently asked, "What part of your piece did you find most interesting to do?" or "What part would you improve?" The students did respond in a more thoughtful way than in the beginning of my study with them. When asked the part they'd improve, almost every child thoughtfully reflected, then commented. Our classroom was becoming a place where children really noticed the signs of interested and engaged learners. I saw an increased investment in the quality of their own and others' work. Notes showed up in the Grapevine Box which said, "Jay helped me to critique my writing and suggested I change the ending and make it shorter." "Steven helped Kevin arrange the backdrop in

PETER WRENN

his diorama." "Megan showed Sarah the book she was reading and said that she will bring in another book from home by the same author for Sarah to read."

It Must Have Taken You a Long Time

The benefit from concentrating on critiquing showed up clearly on the day that students began to represent the maritime projects they had been working on for the past three weeks. The projects were a culmination of a lengthy study we had undertaken, beginning with a trip to the Norwalk Maritime Center and the underwater research Jason Project we had studied.

During the project, I had noticed children helping each other to a greater degree than ever before, asking more in-depth "critiquing" questions like "Where did you find this information?" or "Why did you choose this color?" They felt free to make suggestions: "I think you should color all in one direction because that looks better" or "You could make your shark out of clay and it will stand out then." I noticed some students reworking parts of projects based on these exchanges.

Ian, however, had finished his project quickly and, even with some questioning by me, could not determine *anything* else that could be done to enhance it. I was convinced that this boy knew that this was not a project that showed his ability, much less his interest! But he was eager to be done, and content to continue sitting. I prodded further:

"What part of your project are you most interested in?"

"Drawing the pictures from one scene to the other," came the response.

"How many pictures do you have?"

"Six."

"Considering that we have at least five more days to work on our projects, what could you do to improve your project?"

"Nothing."

"I notice that the pictures are all pencil sketches. What could you do to make them more interesting, to show all the details?"

"I could color them, but I don't wanna. I like them this way." A challenging look was directed at me.

"Have you checked with your critiquing partner?"

"Yes, and he wants me to color, and add more features."

"And you've chosen to . . . ?"

The challenging look escalated to quiet defiance. "I like it this way, and I'm gonna leave it."

A bit frustrated, I made a decision here to watch and observe over the next few days. If necessary, I would step in and help Ian re-focus and demand that he put more time and effort into his project.

The next day he sat during choice time, then picked up his project, flipped through it, and put it away. He engaged in conversation with students at his cluster, pointing out which students needed to improve things. His comments were helpful and accurate, and many students accepted the critiquing with ease, gave the comments some thought, and did make additions and corrections. Ian, nevertheless, did not choose to add any work to his own project. Over the next couple of days I continued to observe. Sometimes Ian chose to read a science book; sometimes he talked with others about their work. He did not return to his own project.

Then arrived the day students began representing their work. The first project was a diorama showing sharks and their eating habits. To show that the sharks do not sleep, the student chose to suspend his clay models by thin strings. They really seemed to move through the exquisitely detailed background. His research was of high quality, and, as this student fielded questions about his work, it was clear that he was proud of it.

Next representation: This student had involved others in helping her act out a scene from an underwater habitat. She wrote the script, made the props, directed the skit. All the information was factual, some of it quite amazing! Her classmates excitedly formulated questions that they really wanted answered, prompted by her presentation. The comments they made showed clearly their appreciation of the work she had done. I watched Ian's face as he raised his hand to be recognized. "Your project is awesome! It must have taken you a really long time."

Immediately afterward Ian came up to me. "Can I do another project, Ms. Kaplan? I don't like the way mine came out."

"Is there something you could do to fix it?" I asked.

"No, I don't like it. I want to forget all about it and start again."

"Why?" I wondered.

"I don't like it, and I can do better."

Yes! I thought to myself, what a breakthrough! "But, Ian," I proceeded cautiously, "we are into the representing phase of our projects. How long will it take you to do a quality project?"

"I'll work at home and in school. I should be able to finish in two or three days. I know just how I'll do it, Ms. Kaplan. I can do it. I really can!"

Ian was pleading to work hard. I savored the moment. "When did you realize you wanted to do another project?"

"When I saw the other kids' projects."

This seemed a shining moment for both of us. I was thrilled that Ian chose to improve his work, that he saw the need for improvement. I was particularly pleased that he recognized and commented upon the effort of his classmate. "It must have taken you a long time."

Wasn't That Boring?

By late spring conversation about boring situations and "unboring" ourselves crept in around many edges of our classroom, not just in the structures I set up. I saw this as a very positive sign that students had sincerely become invested in this issue and were chewing on it. One Monday at Morning Meeting, Gina reported on a lengthy Graduation for her older sister that she had attended that weekend. College graduation ceremonies were not something that most of the students had experience or knowledge of, and interest was keen.

"It lasted for hours?" asked Joe incredulously. "Wasn't that boring?"

"Well, not at first," replied Gina, "but after a while, kinda."

Martin's hand went up. "How did you unbore yourself?" came the question.

I couldn't believe it. Every student was listening, poised, really interested in the answer.

"I read the program," answered Gina seriously. "I picked some of the big last names and tried to see how many other words I could make out of them."

Yes! I let out a silent cheer. We had made it!

Taking it One Step Further

Just before the end of the year we had two terrific meetings when we shared what we had learned about ourselves and about becoming involved with learning. The sharing was honest and thoughtful. "The Boring Book showed me what other people thought was boring. I couldn't believe it. Some people even thought Disney World was boring! I'm glad we got to think of solutions!"

Another commented, "I learned that boring is not just 'not doing something.' Sometimes you're bored when you're doing something like swimming. I learned to make myself take it one step further—like using diving rings and seeing how long it takes to pick them up."

One holdout disclosed, "I know what it means when I want to say I'm bored, but I still maybe don't want to do anything about it!"

Though he might not be willing to let on, I had seen grudging movement toward pride in his work even from this boy. Certainly his awareness had been raised—no small step, I told myself.

We celebrated our accomplishments by proving that we could be really engaged in activity for 10 minutes, working up to 20 minutes. The rules of the activity as stated by the class were: the activity must be done by yourself, quietly; and, once you chose an activity you must stick with it for the duration. Some chose to read; some colored; some wrote; some chose to sit and think. All remarked at the end that reaching the goal was easy. We could have gone on to new time limits had the school year not ended.

What We All Strive To Be!

Though these students will move on to another room, another teacher, I'm not ready to let go of this topic yet. I feel as if I have just begun to scratch the surface and there are so many directions I could take it. Next year I plan to state my clear positive for the class very early on. They will know that I want all of them to be active, engaged learners. I will help them in any way that I can, but I will make sure that the students understand that each of us is responsible for taking care of those moments when we feel bored, to find positive solutions. I'll more aggressively guide those who say they don't want to, or can't, engage. I'd also like to spend more time observing those children who can sit idly for blocks of time but don't say they're bored. How are they able to remain unbored? What are they thinking?

This was a great experience for my class and me. I learned so much about the students, the process of engaging in your own education, and about my own expectations for kids. Every step of the process made me appreciate teaching. I find myself noticing people who are engaged in their jobs and other pursuits everywhere. Several friends shared with me how valuable this study has been for *them*. We agree that engaged, active learners are what we all strive to be.

RUTH'S COMMENTARY *Unbore Yourself*

> "I want to give children an allowance—allow them time to imagine, to expand, and to grow. For this to happen they have to become invested in their education. . . . It won't happen if they're bored."
>
> —Colette Kaplan

There is a story that Colette related over the phone which never made it into the final case study, yet it seems so telling. It is one of those end-of-year moments which often show in unexpected ways what our children internalize and understand from the year's curriculum. This example came from the teacher's sharing a weekend adventure at the

Morning Meeting circle. Colette had taken her own children to see the passing of the Olympic Torch. She described the crowds and the tension of the moment as all waited . . . and waited. Her students quickly reacted with questions, some of which had less bearing on the historical moment than on one of the year's topics of study:

Student One: Did you get bored waiting?
Colette: No, I did not.
Student Two: OK. But did your kids get bored?

These fifth grade students confront the issue of boredom this year. The study grows out of experience with boredom—or what they call boredom. As part of their investigation they discuss and list causes. They propose strategies to "unbore themselves." They put strategies into actions, posting observations in their Grapevine Box, assembling a book of tactics to unbore, and practicing challenge activities. They celebrate the accomplishment of first ten and then twenty minutes of self-initiated, sustained time on a not-boring task. They feel ready to go longer when the year ends!

Here is yet another indicator that the question posed by the teacher is also becoming a question posed by the student. It is no longer taken for granted that to stand and wait has to be boring. The very question asked suggests that it is indeed possible to wait and yet not be bored—doubtful, curious, but possible. And it seems to me that one of the most important things a teacher can do is to plant those seeds of possibility.

"But did your kids get bored?" My guess is that they did not, because they had been swept up not only by the energy of the crowd, but also by their mother's eagerness. It is contagious, after all. And so is the converse, the sweep of disengaged learners. As we continually see in our own classrooms and through the windows provided by these case studies, the best programs are not always enjoyed by our students. We can create a feast and find that no one eats it. Even if most come and take part, we worry about those who hold back, say they are not hungry, complain that there is actually nothing on the table. Colette Kaplan's one year study provides a fascinating glimpse into not just the panoply of why children say they are bored, but also direct interventions which bring children to the table, their own table. What we see in this study is how the children's appetites for engagement are kindled. Boredom goes from being a staple to being a problem to becoming a challenge and even an interesting question, a topic to investigate.

This case looks at particular individuals who repeatedly complain they are "bored." It also looks at the expectations of the classroom community. It demonstrates that as the culture of the classroom changes, some of the more reluctant individuals do as well. We see this in the report about Ian, who withstands the teacher's nudging to improve his underwater project yet responds to the "awesome work" of peers. It is also significant that Ian identifies hard work rather than skill or talent as the critical element in his classmate's achievement: "It must have taken you a long time," he comments.

Colette has built class expectations that value real work. In Eileen's study, she introduces the concept of real talk. Here I think we might consider "real work" as a functioning attribute. Real work takes many forms. A common aspect of real work is that it requires effort. Whether it involves children with math difficulties, children who need to extend project work, or students who are frustrated by a design that just won't work, the common underlying variable is effort.

Colette observes Anna and Claudia cease working on the Native American diorama after only a short time with little intention of continuing. They are done, they say. She observes Samantha hide from her math work. In her journal she notes that a group of girls give up after several attempts to make their log cabin hold together. In each case, prompted by a myriad of causes, children withdraw their participation. Colette notes that this occurs not just when the tasks are teacher directed, part of the assigned curriculum. This also occurs during "choice" time. In this fifth grade class hands-on projects are a large part of each social studies unit. With each project, students choose a topic of interest to research and represent to their classmates. For example, Anna and Claudia have chosen to work on dwellings when they are discovered idle and bored. Even the opportunity to explore their personal interests results in disgruntled and nonproductive students. Effort ceases during a required math period; effort ceases during a choice work period. "It's boring," as the student/teacher discussion reveals, covers a multitude of situations, with the consistent consequence that effort stops.

When effort stops, in effect, children give up. In tackling the issue of "boredom" Colette insists that children find a way back to their work and to high quality outcomes. It is interesting that as these children return to their tasks, we do see higher quality outcomes. Effort, according to a recent Carnegie report, *Years of Promise* (1996), appears to be a significant determinant for school success. Effort also stands out in the anecdotal evidence of the classroom. I have often marveled at how well some of my students with learning disabilities seem to do as they get older. It is as if they have gotten the message about working hard. They have learned that effort matters. I recall a time when my third grade class had just come back from a pond study and the children were set to record experiences. Megan scowled and glared at a blank sheet of paper. A very bright but timid, almost prissy child, she had held back, watching while others sank their feet or hands into the dirt and water. "It's boring," she had announced. In fact, she was able to see that her reluctance to get her feet wet had deprived her of the fun and excitement of the experience. She had been afraid. On the next excursion we knew we needed to practice putting fingers into the water, turning over rocks, and gently holding newts. As others gathered around to see Megan's finds on that trip, the shine on her face was indeed not boring. Megan was receptive. Unfortunately not all children will be so receptive so quickly. This year I observe quite a number who lash out against "boring" science or "boring" writing— the very subjects they find hard.

The good news is that effort is fluid and flexible while other variables may be more fixed and innate. We can try to help students discover their own aptitudes to invest themselves in a task. To help children become willing to do the hard work is truly one of the more nagging and complex tasks we face. That it is possible seems all the more evident from this case study.

Colette writes, "I want to give children an allowance—allow them time to imagine, to expand, and to grow. For this to happen they have to become invested in their education. . . . It won't happen if they're 'bored.'"

Colette approaches this problem first by observing and naming the problem. Next she involves her students in a change process "to unbore" themselves. A moment about phrase mongering. I often find that children do embrace an apt phrase. Often it is a metaphor which provides a way for them to visualize doing and behaving in a different way. "Step on your brakes" and "Use that power steering" help children who are struggling to find some impulse control. The notion of "de-cliquing" rallied my older students to a better state of awareness and action. I once handed out "homework licenses" for those who passed the "road test" of showing they could handle the skills of independent work. Indeed I borrowed heavily from the driving metaphor, with a road test, a written manual and the final allocation of little plastic cards to be carried at all times! The phrase "unbore yourself" is such a technique. It names an expectation. It provides a common language and even specialness; it involves the students as collaborators in their learning. We see from the teacher's report that the word does grab them. They enjoy that it is an invention. And it signifies: un-bore/not bore. A verb, an action. If you are not bored, what will you do?

"Unbore yourself" begins the process of imagining an alternative possibility. The teacher develops a new expectation, one that implies an active rather than passive response. By adding the word "yourself," she suggests to the students that they play a key role. The very thing that they cease to do—engage—they will have to do to unbore. What a problem!

Throughout this case, Colette shares and engages her students in the problem. She creates a balance between teacher and student re-sponsibility. She does not solve the construction problem for her frus-trated girls but instead helps them identify appropriate sources of help. She offers to make a special time to work with Samantha on her math. Clearly, she has raised the level of interest of all her children in the "beast called Boredom" and tapped their potential to take a serious look at what is, after all, boring.

It is also important to acknowledge that school (like real life) is com-prised of a range of tasks. Some involve intellectual, physical and cre-ative capacities, as in the example of building the large scale log cabin. This task, which becomes a measure of high engagement, results in a sense of class pride which the children derive both from the challeng-ing process and the final product. Not all things that happen in school will be or should be as demanding. To renew and sustain our energies requires a balance of activity. I certainly find that after a job of writ-ing I long to rake the leaves or sort the laundry. Too much domestic ordering makes me crave my writing again. I have seen from hindsight that days which are too filled with choices leave children drained and tense. Equally, days which are all routine and busy work create a tedium and restless energy. After working hard on a science experiment how happily I see the children pick up their spelling workbooks and quietly copy word lists. Colette makes it clear that not everything will be up to the "log cabin" caliber. Not every piece of work takes several drafts or lengthy deliberations. There is satisfaction to be gained from the effort to master facts, to achieve accuracy, to go through the repetitive motions that stacking wood, chopping carrots or achieving good penmanship may require.

When I go back and read the lists made up by the children about what boring means, I am again struck by how many different elements there are to understand and manage. I see on that list the item "rushing." I think about how important time can be to do a job well, even to just settle in properly. I observe my own students dash through room clean-up jobs in a mad race to get done and out to the soccer field. I see Rosa who is not going to soccer still arranging the colored paper and crayons on the shelf making them all tidy and pretty. And it is rather ironic that often the trumpet call that gets the teacher's attention is seeing children not using time well. Colette begins her quest with the two girls who have "finished" and are sitting with nothing to do. We see how children fail to fill the time, but often miss that we fail to give the time.

The student list for causes of boring has other seemingly contradictory definitions (too hard/too easy; out of ideas/don't want to). Given such variation and complexity, it would take indeed a superteacher to always get the ingredients just right for one student, never mind twenty-five. In other words, we must be able to observe and individualize. There will always be a need to engage children in conversations concerning how they can unbore themselves. We need to help them look at their own reluctance or resistance and teach them to ask themselves the questions: Is this too hard? Do I not care? Do I not know how to extend this work? Am I stuck? This process of questioning is also relevant to the methods of critique which children use as they share their projects.

I want to say a few more words about critiquing since it is a fairly new classroom method and although it takes time to teach and time to do, it has an important impact on the quality of work children do. I learned about critiquing from two sources. First I learned from "work representing," a technique articulated by High Scope Educational Research Foundation in the 1970s. Representing was a way for children to share their work in an interactive setting. The focus was on developing skills of specific appreciation. Children were encouraged to notice detail and effort. The author or artist briefly read or told about a facet of her work. "Questions or comments?" she then asked. Children were encouraged to respond with examples of things they noticed and liked, telling why. They were encouraged to ask questions about how or why. "How did you get the figures to stand up?" "I noticed that you made the sky purple. Was that how it looked or did you have a different reason?" Representing encouraged children to value and learn from each other's work. It also improved language and critical thinking skills.

In recent years I have also learned more about critiquing from the work of a colleague, Ron Berger, who teaches sixth grade in Shutesbury, Massachusetts.[3] He has been one of a number of teachers inventing and reinventing the practice of critique. Listening to Ron, it is clear that critique has helped his students revise their drafts and extend the quality of their work. He takes time every year to instruct and prepare students to observe carefully, comment respectfully and value their own and each other's efforts. It is particularly moving to see the progress and pride of students with special needs who willingly share a first draft which is far more rudimentary than their peers' work.

I have also adapted a form of critique which I introduce in the beginning of the year. My seventh and eighth grade students create a poster of a summer reading book they wish to promote. They spend a week working on these posters. They think about a catchy blurb, the use of color and design and choose realistic or abstract illustrations. I lobby for no white in the background. When they are done, we critique. Critiquing for us is not about fault finding. I tell them, "Critiquing is the art or skill of making discriminating judgments or comments." We get into energetic discussions of what is to be learned from this poster's dominant colors, central images, dark or light moods, and suggestive words. Then one day I send the students off to critique the posters with a partner. I see them sit silently for a while and then as they go to work I am struck by how serious and thoughtful they are and what it might mean to take such care with the work they have produced.

It is clear that critiquing is an effective method in Colette's room. We see her pride in her students and their growing pride in each other. Colette notes that the process of questioning specifics is becoming spontaneous. "During the project, I noticed children helping each other to a much greater degree, asking more in-depth questions." Colette also notes how the critiquing session enables Ian to move from reluctance to excitement as he enjoys the "awesome" work of his peers.

In summary, this case offers a number of critical interventions that help children to engage in their work with more success and to take an interest in the task of "unboring themselves." These interventions evolve organically, in bits and pieces, spontaneously and through careful planning. There is not really an invariable sequence or order, except for the naming perhaps. The following list reviews some of the elements that helped Colette:

1. Using class discussions to identify the various meanings of the word "boring"
2. Identifying the clear positive of "unboring yourself"
3. Noticing and reinforcing efforts to unbore yourself
4. Introducing the method of critiquing as a way to expand and share work
5. Setting up a measure of "engagement"—based on the positive experience of hard work (log cabin measure)
6. Creating a challenge activity of "unboring yourself" for ten minutes, then twenty minutes
7. Reinforcing other needs when children feel bored—noticing individual struggles

Does this mean that children will never be bored or that they should never be allowed to feel bored? No. It is not possible because there is a dynamic relationship between teacher, learner, content and time. I go back to Colette's clear positive to give her children an allowance. I believe that all our children need this allowance. They all need time to imagine, to expand, and to grow. For that they will need to harness effort and to unbore themselves.

CHAPTER EIGHT

MOVING THE TEACHER'S DESK

Democracy in a Fifth/Sixth Grade

by Dottie McCaffrey

PETER WRENN

Dorothy McCaffrey is a graduate of Emmanuel College in Boston where she majored in English. After a brief stint as an English and Latin teacher in a suburban junior high school, she stayed at home for eleven years with her children. Before moving to western Massachusetts, she worked in day care on the North Shore. She returned to teaching twenty-four years ago in western Massachusetts and has spent those years working with grades five and six, except for five years in grades three and four. Her graduate work was done at the University of Massachusetts at Amherst, where she earned a master's degree in education with a concentration in Integrated Day. She is the mother of three adult children and enjoys reading, gardening and traveling in her leisure time.

The fifteen fifth and sixth graders had arranged their tables in a large circle. They were anxiously waiting to see whose role they would play in the historical simulation they were about to begin. For several days we had been using documents from the Plymouth Plantation archives to study the Puritans' religious and political beliefs as background reading for the novel *The Witch of Blackbird Pond*. We drew names. Amy, a pleasant, dutiful student who had avoided leadership roles in school until now, chose the name of John Carver, the governor of the colony. It would be her role to lead the meeting that was the subject of the simulation. The setting was the *Mayflower* where the Pilgrims and their non-Pilgrim fellow travelers were to make the rules that would guide their behavior once they reached the New World.

Amy smiled shyly but confidently as the others continued to draw names. I wondered if she was up to such a demanding task, but resigned myself to the role I had assumed for the lesson—secretary. The discussion began. Amy conducted the meeting with fairness and confidence. She mediated disagreements diplomatically, led the group to consensus, and called for votes as discussion wound down. The children responded by taking turns, listening to each other, and staying in their roles. Even Eliot, whose tendency toward arguing often disrupted class, stayed in character. They concluded after an hour and a half with a list of rules that demonstrated their grasp of the Puritans' world view. It reflected ideas in the *Mayflower Compact* that the Pilgrims themselves created almost four hundred years ago, but which the class had not yet read.

This is the kind of lesson that makes me glad that I am a teacher. Not only do I enjoy the way primary source material prepares children for understanding history; I also highly value teaching the roles civil discourse and democracy have played in shaping the different cultures we study. As I basked in the success of this lesson I was struck by how rarely these same students, who so effectively argued, discussed, reasoned and compromised as Pilgrims, took such roles in our own daily classroom discourse. I wanted our classroom to follow these same ideals of democracy and active participation. The problem was how to achieve this.

That day, thinking about why so few students actively participated and how reluctant students seemed to be about choosing to pursue particular topics in their academic work, I mulled over possible factors that might be contributing to the problem. For the last several years I have wondered whether the physical environment could be inhibiting participation in classroom decisions and discussions. After discussing these concerns with Ruth this year, I wondered again whether changing the way I managed the physical space and organization of the materials might invite the children to participate more. Perhaps it would help if I included them more in decisions about the classroom, such as how and where we store materials, what should be available, how we care for supplies, and how we design our work space and bulletin board. Changing the classroom might also help me reorient my teaching. I remembered how I changed my outlook when I broke my leg several years ago and had to remain seated for several months. My change in position required a change in what I did and how I did it. I also thought about this community of children.

The school where I teach is a pre-kindergarten through sixth grade school in a rural mill town. The mills are declining but many parents still have "working class" jobs. Outside cultural influences come primarily from the television, from sports and from school trips to museums, cities, and theater. Few parents are educated beyond high school and many remember their own schooling as an unpleasant experience. I work hard to strengthen the sense of community in my class through daily Morning Meetings and I often call Class Meetings to solve problems. Each year I introduce them to ancient cultures so they can become connected not only to their classmates, but also to people in other times and places. I introduce them to communities that have exercised tolerance and we compare them with those that haven't. We consider the price of taking difficult ethical stands and weigh the outcomes against cultures that have chosen differently. I make a point of integrating discussions about ethics into academics to augment our social curriculum. As we read and discuss historical literature, the children meet memorable characters and address life issues that many might not otherwise have considered.

Throughout the school, teachers provide rich curricula. But in spite of this, the children often are not engaged as fully as they might be. They rarely go beyond the required material or become truly engrossed in their studies. I wondered why. I thought again about my discussion with Ruth. Perhaps what they needed most was an opportunity to practice taking a more active role in decisions that would affect their own school experience. Rearranging the physical space might offer an opportunity for them to exercise some real responsibility and maybe take some ownership of our classroom. Perhaps this would lead to a more successful Choice Time.

I resolved to work on the physical organization of our classroom in concert with my students. I introduced my plan after Christmas vacation. The first day back in January, I put all of the tables askance and wrote on the message board that the class could arrange the room as they liked and sit where they wanted. There was a buzz of excitement and a flurry of activity. The class immediately divided into two kinds of groups: those who grabbed a buddy and sat down where a table was without moving it (Rachel and Terri, Eliot and Pete) and those who had a grand plan that they tried to convince others was the best. The planners couldn't budge the sitters, so they worked among themselves to arrange, discuss and rearrange around the sitters. Sean arranged a table, sat on it and kept trying to get others to join him. Although he had a good idea, no one listened to him. He just talked into the air without directly addressing anyone. It was only that day after having taught him for a year and a half that I realized that he really didn't understand that if he wanted to communicate an idea, he had to make sure he had listeners. He wouldn't approach the group, but kept trying to talk to them. After about twenty minutes, the class settled into seats that they kept for several weeks.

Over the next few days, I conducted class discussions in which I told the children that I wanted to hear their ideas about what a good school needs to have. During the first session, I asked them to brainstorm what a perfect classroom needs. The following list contains the ideas that they generated:

The Perfect Classroom Needs
learners
a likable teacher
familiar classmates
interesting subjects
students who pay attention
good equipment—books, computers
good furniture setup
appropriately-sized furniture
a variety of teachers for different subjects
a safe school structure

Then we discussed what the purpose of school should be. They mentioned learning academics, learning how to pay attention and show good manners, and learning how to be around other people.

That night I thought about our discussion. I noted sadly that in neither discussion did any child mention the importance of being able to choose a topic or activity. I also noticed that this list reflected the children's need to be protected and taught by the adults around them. Satisfying that need while showing them how to be more independent was the task at hand. The children were somewhat reticent during the discussion and I remembered longingly the lesson in which they had role played the Pilgrims. Why couldn't they take the same active roles in class that they had taken in their discussions as Pilgrims? Perhaps they needed more experience in decision making. I decided to begin immediately giving them more experience.

In the next discussion I shared with them what I wanted physically to happen in the room and invited them to help decide how we could best achieve these things together. My list included the following:

enough physical space for every child to work comfortably
storage space for children's possessions
a place for the coat cabinet
an art and project area
a cooking area
a science table
a convenient place for games so they would be used
a place for cubbies
places for reading books, reference books, theme books for so-
    cial studies and science
a place for writing materials
a place for the computer

Their immediate response was, "We don't have enough room to do all that!" I had originally planned to let the discussion "cook" for a few days before assigning the task of designing the room plans but the next day, two children, Sam and Mary, took the initiative and brought in room plans. We began to change the room around according to Mary's plan, which reoriented where the tables faced. This required my using chart paper on the wall for some lessons since there was no blackboard on that side of the room. I did enjoy the chance to experiment with a different side of the room being the "front." Several children were concerned that this plan might not leave a good space for our Morning Meeting circle because the table arrangement used too much space, so we made a minor alteration to fit our meeting oval. Mary also assigned who sat where, allowing for, I soon realized, what she knew to be the preferences of her classmates.

After a few days, I noticed that the children were definitely not doing their best work in Mary's seating assignments. I began to see sloppiness increasing in all the written work and heard an undercurrent of constant talking and grumbling. We had a meeting in which I said that I felt they needed to branch out, that they were too comfortable in their spots, and their work and behavior were suffering as a result. I told them about the learning curve and how we often needed to be made uncomfortable with something before we would develop the im-

Today in class, we changed seats... so I'm not sitting next to Sandy any more, I'm sitting by Bob. I guess it's Ok, it doesn't really matter to me. Besides, I think I sit next to Sandy too much

Mary

Bob

This morning in class we changed seats. We changed them because people were comfortable with the people they were sitting next to and they weren't doing their work. They were chatting and not paying attention. I'm glad that we changed seats. I'm glad because you can get to know other people. I've never sat beside Mary.

petus to learn. In an attempt to "make the familiar strange," a phrase I remembered from graduate school, I told them I planned to make them a bit uncomfortable so they could learn some new social skills. I asked them to trust that taking new seats would be a positive experience. After rearranging them, I asked them to write about the experience. They seemed agreeable about the changes and I noticed that they seemed happy to work and talk with each other politely. In fact, I think they welcomed a chance to do what they were too shy to do on their own—work with new people.

After one week, we discussed what we liked about Mary's plan. Everyone liked the fact that the tables were arranged in a pattern that allowed "walking space" around the room. They all liked that arrangement itself although they suggested minor adjustments, such as moving the coat cabinet inside the room and rearranging some other furniture. Finally, they moved their chairs to the opposite side of each table to reverse the side of the room that served as the "front." We decided to try this for another week before giving Sam's plan a whirl.

A second discussion of Mary's plan the next week was very flat and uninformative. As I tried to discuss her plan with them, I realized that they lacked the skills to talk about this project. I needed to teach them how to say what they thought in a positive way. They then could figure out a polite way to tell me how they really felt about the room arrangements.

We next arranged the room according to Sam's plan. His design organized the tables and chairs in a rectangle, open at one end. This gave a wonderful space in the middle of the room for Morning Meeting. We decided where the storage furniture should be, but we still had not come up as a group with ideas for placing materials. Mary and Sam volunteered to spend two recesses organizing markers, paper, crayons, games and other materials. Their arrangement proved to be accessible and easy to keep in order. The whole class appreciated their work, especially their periodic efforts to "neaten up" the supplies. Unfortunately, Sam's plan, like Mary's, was not perfect. It became immediately apparent that Eliot and Kevin were now in prime spots for showing off. They began making faces at and comments about others, and because everyone could see them all the time, they became the focal point of the room. Even children who normally ignored them willingly attended to them now. This arrangement also gave Pete a bird's eye view of everyone in the room, which inspired him to provide a commentary on the behavior of the whole class.

Sam's plan lasted only one week. After discussing its obvious drawbacks privately with Sam and then with the class, I proposed a slightly different room arrangement based on their ideas. Because we were beginning a unit about Greece organized around learning teams, we arranged clusters of tables where three or four children could work together. After several weeks we discussed this arrangement's merits. The consensus was that they liked this setup. They appreciated having several people to interact with and they enjoyed having more elbow room. A few who complained about being stuck at the corner of the table or having to share with a space hog discovered they could remedy the situation by simply repositioning their chairs. It made me a little sad to realize that, in spite of all my efforts to empower them to make decisions and take responsibility, they still felt they needed my permission to move their chairs. To make more room, we decided to move the large work tables and return the coat cabinet to the hall now that they wore less outer gear. In response to complaints from those whose cubbies were near the floor, several children volunteered to swap. Was altruism taking hold?

Terri decided that I should get rid of my desk since I never sat at it and it took up so much room. I conceded both points, but explained that I needed a private place to keep records, my lunch and clerical paraphernalia. The kids were unconvinced and suggested alternate storage places. I felt I needed to keep the desk in the room, but I moved it as far into a corner as it would go. I realized that this suggestion was daring coming from them and appreciated the spunk involved in their making it. They were definitely becoming more involved in the space issue and more willing to pursue discussion.

From the beginning of my experimenting with room arrangements two of my goals had been for the children to make more choices about the topics they would pursue and to participate more actively. As the Greek unit got underway with its group decision-making component and many art projects, I was pleased to see more choice occurring. The children selected a greater variety of materials for their projects and the new central organization helped them keep the room neater as they

PETER WRENN

worked. The groups were even functioning as I had hoped—not all as complete democracies, but at least with the consent of their members.

In May, I initiated another activity designed to illustrate the importance of civil discourse. Our final activity in the Greek unit was to study some famous speeches. The first was Pericles' speech in praise of Athens. They read the speech, studied it in their small groups, and listed what they thought was important. Then we discussed the points as a class, focusing on how the Greeks' values affected their lives. We compared the Greeks' values with those of the Pilgrims and the Quakers whom we had studied earlier and we talked about how our school and class had rules based on our values. Next we studied two of Socrates' speeches—his defense at his trial and his speech reminding the Athenians of the values they were betraying by sentencing him to death. The children showed a wonderful understanding of what had happened and how it connected to the politics and conditions of the time. Participation was consistently enthusiastic, often mimicking the spirit of debate and intensity one imagines in a Greek marketplace.

As I look back on the problem I chose to work on, I wonder if our discussions about the room changed the students' involvement or if their interest in and love of the Greek unit inspired more participation in the class. I don't know. It is one of the fascinations of teaching that the interplay of factors requires so much thought. Only by reflecting about and working out problems do we learn. Did the discussions about furniture placement and supplies cause changes that worked for them? Certainly our own classroom now better reflected the Greek ideals we were discussing. Perhaps as children thought out loud about Greek democratic ideals they were reminded of similar moments in their own room. Did the focus on physical environment change my point of view? I think it did. Although I have had many room arrangements over the years, I discovered some new orientations this year. Letting the kids arrange the supplies showed me that my previous organization had prevented accessibility to materials and interfered with their proper care.

Of course, not everything fell in place immediately. Three room arrangements and many small adjustments after we began, we finally settled on solutions that worked well for us. Perhaps it was the need to keep discussing and keep trying that really engendered greater participation and the feeling that everyone's ideas counted. I'll never know for sure.

By introducing more democracy into our classroom decisions, I tried to connect their own choices to the intellectual material they were trying to understand. I see now that maybe these two strands—how we run our classrooms and what we study in those classrooms—need to be more connected.

I learned again, as I do every year, that it is my job to teach children how to become more involved in their learning, whether it is through discussing our classroom space or by introducing them to the wider world of learning they otherwise might not have experienced. My curriculum is tailored to convey facts and to encourage curiosity. For me this is the ultimate democracy—to offer them models for how to engage in and appreciate the wider culture beyond our small rural town and to give them the tools necessary to participate in that culture, from reading books and surfing the Internet to knowing how to treat others and how to discuss issues. But we cannot teach the ethics of democracy without giving them opportunities to experience real democracy in the daily operations of their lives. By introducing more democracy into our classroom decisions, I tried to connect their own choices to the intellectual material they were trying to understand. I see now that maybe these two strands—how we run our classrooms and what we study in those classrooms—need to be more connected. Active participation grows when it can be concretely practiced within the confines of our room. Questions about furniture arrangement started us in the right direction.

Participating in a project designed to look at how teachers introduce change has forced me to reflect on my work and to document those reflections in a way I never would have without the impetus of the assignments and deadlines they imposed. At this time in what is the autumn of my career, I have come away with a renewed desire to continue to ask myself questions and to spend each year answering them.

RUTH'S COMMENTARY *Moving the Teacher's Desk*

I will explore two questions in relation to this case study:

1. What is the relationship of the academic to the social curriculum in a classroom for older students?
2. What is the meaning and value of "choice" in upper grades?

By focusing on room arrangement, Dottie McCaffrey gives her fifth and sixth graders a concrete place to start exploring choice in their room. As I observe the children struggle with this particular assignment, I find myself drawn into a neat partnership of social and academic learning. The principles of democracy and civil exchange studied in the history curriculum give context and value to their own class meeting agendas. Where should the desks go? What is a good seating arrangement? Why isn't this plan working? Their specific attempts to design their own space seem to guide them to identify with rather than distance themselves from historical abstractions.

When Dottie first begins this study she carefully identifies herself as a teacher who loves her subject matter. She takes pride in her ability to engage her students in history, geography, literature and to relate content to current interests. She uses her passions for learning and knowledge of content to construct projects and lively classroom activity. She translates concepts of the past into role-playing in the present.

In her case study, Dottie seeks to implement greater "choice." Choice, she hopes, will increase students' involvement in their studies. She seems initially to differentiate choice from the ongoing academic work of the classroom. Yet, she hopes for greater student initiative connected to the curriculum. She embraces two aims—to teach subject matter knowledge and to teach ways of being in the world. She has faith that a knowledge of the past will help students grasp a more democratic present. She wants to encourage students to become those citizens Socrates would have admired. The first aim she advances with ease and confidence. The second—her desire to encourage greater participation—reveals her willingness to risk, to ask new questions, to experiment along with her students.

Often as teachers struggle with issues of student initiative and accountability they think about choice. We need to find approaches that permit children to participate in real ways in their education. That does not mean we must individualize everyone's own contract, program, or schedule. Rather, we must help children feel less marginal in the classroom. When people feel marginal, they become more reticent. It is important to give students systematic input into what they learn. This is especially critical if we want them to begin to regard school as a place where they can express their ideas and show initiative.

Many things have changed since I started teaching, yet a permanent fixture for me has been to see how much children learn when treated to the passionate knowledge of a teacher. Twenty-five years ago I watched a master teacher in a Harlem first grade ready her students for reading. All she had was one of those old-fashioned basals where Dick and Jane do their thing. Yet this teacher turned cardboard characters into fascinating friends and the books into a treasury of delicious words. Clearly, her love of reading and her desire for her children to read transcended the material. It was a vital lesson to realize how important the ability to impart knowledge and a love of learning are for education. Therefore, to create a context for participation is not to give over but to give. Dottie McCaffrey invites her students to share her love of learning history.

Dottie seizes on choice as one vehicle for increased participation. As teachers begin to envision choice, room organization plays an inevitable role in the change process. Materials need to be accessible. Children need to be able to find and get what they need without a lot of commotion. They need to be able to move. They need to be able to work together. And they need some parameters for what is possible.

In the beginning of this case study, the students struggle with room arrangement in something of a vacuum. Impulse and personality direct decisions. Sean uses his muscles to grab a table, sit on it and try to command others to join him. No one listens to him or his good ideas. Planners cannot oust squatters. Yet the discussions around "purpose of school" and "perfect classroom" provide some information to apply to the task of arranging a room. Looking back at the list, I note that there are several critical ideas suggested such as "getting to know classmates" and "paying attention," as well as tangibles such as furniture and setup. While I am struck by the accuracy of their brainstorming, it is not clear they are drawing a connection between the needs of a perfect classroom and a good room setup. Their first arrangement seems largely to settle friends with friends. We see that at some level the students understand what they need, but do not know how to make those connections or how to put them into practice.

Furthermore, the sharp observations of their teacher show us that while they had conducted their Puritan simulation discussion with finesse, here they stumble over one of the most basic rules of civil discourse—listening to each other. Dottie points out that Sean talks into the air and the planners find they can't budge the sitters and have to work around them. Too many of the children are reticent and do not participate in the discussion the way they had during the Puritan role-playing. Dottie sighs, "Why couldn't they do as themselves what they had done as Pilgrims?" I read these passages and smile, even chuckle out loud. I can just picture the scene. I can also imagine the frustration of the teacher. Why don't even the simple lessons transfer? But then I remember that these lessons are not simple and the connections that we seek between instruction and mastery, between input and output, between concept and doing are never one-to-one. In fact, here is the Piagetian paradigm in the making: children are meaning-makers, but the evolution from assimilation to accommodation, that process of coming to understanding, requires that they act on and interact with real problems. It is often when there is the most disequilibrium, when things are most out of balance, that uneasy learning occurs. That is why the opportunities to choose, to choose wrongly, to rework and to practice become the deep and profound prods for learning, provided that there is structure and a safety net. Structures provide necessary links between the arrangement of the room and the importance of the academic work to be done.

In this case, the teacher employs at least six techniques which provide structure and a safety net:

1. The teacher brings the task to the students. At first she does so physically. Thus, the students must respond in a physically active way. She accepts the first outcome. She then begins to focus them mentally through a series of questions and discussions which she hopes will help to move their thinking and form connections between plans and purposes.

2. The teacher continually observes. She notes how they come to their decisions and observes different students' roles and involvement in the process. She notes the difficulties and listens to their reasoning.

3. The teacher encourages a planning process by accepting the plans that two students bring. Mary explains her plan with teacher help (charting it on the wall) and modifies it with student input after a discussion of the learning curve. Her seating assignments are honored despite teacher trepidation.

4. Teacher interventions, based on ongoing observations and assessments, ensure protection from chaos and harm. When Dottie feels that work and behavior are not acceptable (Sam's plan), she redirects in ways that are respectful and responsive to Sam and the class. I am continually struck by the relationship between where we choose to sit and how we perform. I wonder if the students too were becoming more conscious of this relationship. They were also keeping journals which reveal their growing awareness and investment in the changes. They note that the teacher's intervention helped them to do what they were too shy to do on their own—"get to know other people."

6. The teacher reinforces and also protects student investment

and risk taking. She limits the critique of Mary's plan to positive comments. She encourages student assessment but not at the risk of hurting one another.

As teachers, we need to remember that no one thing works for all students. Mary and Sam, the original planners, volunteer to organize materials. Cubbies, corner tables, and the teacher's desk provoke discussion for other children. I sense that the "daring" nature of suggesting that the teacher move her desk may make it easier for some students to get involved. Wisely, the teacher strikes a compromise on the argument about her desk.

The matter of successful working teams finally takes root when Dottie introduces a new unit in the curriculum. Suddenly the need for choices is apparent. There is a pressing need for centrally located materials, for small group work, for group decisions. Now the groups function as she had hoped.

In this case study classroom decisions parallel a curriculum on democracy that takes fifth and sixth graders into serious content. The content is made accessible through role plays, enactments, carefully selected readings and projects. The children also access the curriculum through the concrete experience of determining aspects of their own classroom life. They too must make choices, and they must come to grips with the implications of these choices.

I come back to the question of choice, asked at the start of this commentary. What is the meaning of choice in classrooms for upper grade students? One answer, offered by this case study, is that a program of choice offers students a role in determining some aspect of their classroom arrangements. We see another aspect towards the end when choice allows students to select topics they are interested in pursuing for their Greek unit. These topics and projects will necessitate team work, access to materials, a room designed to promote productive participation and rich exchange of ideas. Choices made by the plans of one student or the concerted efforts of the whole group influence the very purpose of school. We do have a sense, as does their teacher, that these students, through their choice-making, find ways to pay attention and to "be around new people." We sense that as they shift the physical environment, so they also shift attitudes and ideas and while they never name "choice" as a purpose of school or as necessary to "a perfect classroom," both teacher and students seem to find the process engaging.

Finally, I gain from this case study an answer to the relationship between the social and the academic curriculum. It seems clear to me that they incite each other. A rich curriculum of study is made richer by the concrete social issues of a seating plan. The social curriculum gains depth and meaning through the projects, academic choices and alliance with subject knowledge. I believe that, at best, our social and academic programs do not diverge, but become mutually reinforcing and integrated. We know that the social arrangements can enhance academic learning; we see here that the converse is also true—that academics can enhance and embrace social learning.

COMMON INSIGHTS

AND PROBLEMS

PETER WRENN

PETER WRENN

CHAPTER NINE

COMMON INSIGHTS

"The importance of success in school is profound. A child's fundamental
sense of worth as a person depends substantially on the ability to achieve
in school."

—Carnegie Corporation of New York, *Years of Promise*

Each case study produced important insights in the course of the project. We each discovered techniques which helped the children learn
and approaches which helped the teacher learn. While individual cases
often generated understandings related to the specific case study, a
number of insights can also be generalized from study to study.

LETTING THE SPILL GROW

The concept of judging how much to "let the spill grow" emerges from
Linda Mathews' case study. She articulates a very familiar anxiety. How
long do we wait before stepping in? How much latitude do we give children to explore and attempt on their own? How much mess before we
mobilize? What are the signals that tell us that the spill is growing into
tidal wave proportions? What are the signals that tell us we are simply
uncomfortable with the transition period that often is needed between
our own and our children's action? Linda's study identifies these questions as an important part of the problem-solving process.

Many educators believe a little mess can be instructive. Eleanor
Duckworth describes the need to "mess about" as an essential step in
children's ability to learn to investigate their world. Ellen Doris, in her
essential book, *Doing What Scientists Do*, outlines the careful steps that allow children to move from their wildest guesses to observation, exper-
imentation and serious investigation. The concept of disequilibrium,
used by both Piaget and Gesell, also describes a critical phase when the
inconsistency between preconceptions and an observed reality propels
children to the next phase of learning. Clearly, in the messing-about
phase much learning takes place, especially if children are not left entirely to their own devices. Careful observations are necessary if the
teacher is to know what the children understand, when it is time to re-
teach something and when it is time to add another strategy.

Duckworth (1987) also notes that having wonderful ideas must begin with at least a rudimentary understanding of the material (through learning vocabulary, how to use the equipment, focusing questions, etc.). There is constructive mess and there is destructive mess. The former leads to learning; the latter leads to chaos and tension. When the mess is unproductive and harmful, it is often because a proper foundation has not been established.

Linda Mathews lays a proper foundation by setting up structures, like her spill team, which permit and encourage practice. In each of the case studies, teachers provides such structures—structures which

embrace both ritualized and real learning. Sometimes the purpose of the structures is to help build a bridge between the ritualized structures and their transfer into spontaneous situations. I think of my own students, who take part every day in a ceremony of greeting. They shake hands, say hello in Czech, chant and dance, make eye contact and sometimes pass a winsome secret smile. They do it well, usually. Yet only a fraction have internalized greeting as a spontaneous welcome which captures the friendliness and goodness of the community. As I walked into the classroom recently, one of the children approached in a flurry. "I didn't get my assignment yesterday. Do you have another copy?"

"Did I hear a good morning. . . . How are you? Nice to see you, dear teacher," I only partly jest.

It made me wonder. Is it time to let the spill grow? To give them more responsibility? Perhaps they are ready for a greeting team. Or perhaps we might challenge them to offer a friendly greeting to six people they don't usually greet. Transferring the intentional practices of the ritual into their day-to-day behavior will involve letting the spill grow.

Linda creates her "spill teams," a safe and cooperative next step. Arona's class invents a way to share a book. Colette presents her children with the challenge to "unbore themselves," so that even as they play, they answer their own complaints with, "Yes, we know. We know. How will we unbore ourselves!?"

Watching children practice is also often how we know what the children know. I recall watching a six-year-old child, who loved to build, constructing his house with blocks. When I asked if his house had a basement, he pointed to a big space on the top. Observing the gap between his ability to construct and his ability to name informed me that we needed to take a field trip through our building, developing some specific vocabulary. Learning what the children do not know, as Linda demonstrates with the glitter incident, or as Eileen's case study shows with the play dough squabble, helps us perceive instructional holes and examine the possible reasons for them. Why don't the children use real talk, solve problems on their own, say good morning spontaneously? And often we will take the question to the children.

TAKING THE QUESTION TO THE CHILDREN

All the teachers find it useful to "take the question to the children" both as a way to initiate and to extend problem-solving. These group discussions help identify the problem for the children and elicit their ideas. "What makes people bored?" initiates a dynamic class discussion and class involvement in Colette Kaplan's study. "What should we do about sharing the Waldo book?" engages the children in Arona McNeill-Vann's multi-age classroom in a discussion about rules for sharing. Cathy Jacques brings the problem of "play fighting" to her fourth and fifth graders repeatedly through class meetings and writing assignments. We see, in one situation, the beginnings of a new perspective as one child hears, really hears, what another says. We also see sixth graders tackle their room design and watch the project take on meaning as Dottie McCaffrey sharpens her questions and gives the discussion context. In these conversations, problems are shared, identified, named and acted on. They provide a vehicle to gain a student perspective and also lead to a class perspective.

Teachers take questions to the children to accomplish a number of different goals:

1. To develop a common vocabulary and definition (What is play fighting?)
2. To establish shared objectives (Do we want to share?)
3. To decide together on strategies (How will we share, arrange the room, unbore?)
4. To assess and re-evaluate (How is it working? What do *you* notice?)

OBSERVATION

Observation is a key element, both as a diagnostic tool and an assessment tool. It helps teachers clarify the nature of the problem, design solutions, and assess progress and it enables the children to become more aware of the significance of their own actions.

In most cases, observation occurs after the problem is defined. Since an initial sense of a problem often grows out of diffuse concerns, observation helps teachers hone and sharpen their problem statements. "The lunchroom is frantic and noisy." "The transition times are rushed and messy." "The students are fine in classroom but awful the minute they hit the hallways." Observations allow us to go from making judgments to describing specific behavior. They help us focus and narrow the problem. "The problem is not the lunchroom, the problem is the long wait time on the lunch lines. The problem is how to speed up the lines while also teaching kids to wait. Perhaps the problem is also the long intervals between breakfast and lunch."

Observation provides an important link between assumptions and the reality of what actually occurs. We see in "Real Talk" that observation allows Eileen Mariani to see the mechanical way her children have started to use language. Observation shows Linda Mathews that her students repeatedly come to her even though they have a procedure for conflict resolution already set up. Observation reveals to Cathy Jacques "a sneer" that says something isn't working here. Observations show Arona McNeill-Vann that her children want to share,

even the ones who are most possessive and quarrelsome. Observations provide detailed information. They also help teachers see what is working. Linda sits down and records numerous examples of independent problem solving. Dottie observes her students make important decisions and enact choices. Colette sees students unbore themselves even during recess. Eileen observes real talk during spontaneous discussions in her classroom. Observation measures both what doesn't and what does work.

Observation is also a disciplined method of study. It is a time when the objective is to watch the children, to notice and record behavior. Again and again, it surfaces as a key element in the process undertaken here, providing information, clarification and inspiration.

Disciplined observations involve the following:

1. Teacher's primary activity is to observe and record.
2. Observations record actual behavior, not interpreted behavior. ("He grabbed the crayon from Mike" rather than "He is aggressive." Further observations might reveal that Mike is withholding and taunting, that he is the aggressor, in fact.)
3. Observations record specific language.

4. Observations may be shared with students to help them engage in problem solving. They may be reported to students
   as, "I noticed that . . ."

Children can also learn to observe. I was struck by Colette's use of
a "Grapevine Box" for her fifth graders to jot down classroom observations. This is standard procedure for them. Arona also asks her children to observe each other sharing. What a useful technique to help
children see each other in positive ways and also to help them imitate
and learn from each other. I frequently use direct observations to in-
stigate problem solving with my students. "I noticed that on our trip
last Wednesday, there was one group that was telling secrets, making
a lot of noise, standing apart from everyone else. What did you notice?" I find that observations allow the teacher to be more specific and
accurate without being judgmental. This encourages students to respond rather than to defend themselves. It also creates greater self-
awareness. Intentions are harder to use as a starting point. Behaviors
help us establish common perceptions and then we can deal with dif-
fering interpretations.

PLEASANT COLLABORATION AND ETHICAL COACHING

All case study teachers felt an upsurge of conviction as they worked
on their projects, a sense of the moral courage and will needed to face
teaching's challenges. The notion of teacher as ethical coach provided
us with a model. Nel Noddings has stated that the aim of education is
to nurture the ethical ideal and says that "We reveal to him [student]
an attainable image of himself that is lovelier than that manifested in
his present acts. . . . In education, what we reveal to a student about
himself as an ethical and intellectual being has the power to nurture
the ethical ideal or to destroy it." (Noddings, 1984, p. 193) I translate
"the ethical ideal" as the wish to care and to act in a more caring way
in this world. It is a way of being which we can coach as teachers by
nurturing an attitude and an affection for caring in our children.

Arona found a process for this coaching in the notion of "pleasant
collaborations," which she drew from Maslow's work. This process describes how teachers guide children, using the wisdom and protection
of their authority while also knowing and respecting the children. The

teacher is the authority without being authoritarian. While "working jointly," one dictionary definition of collaboration, is key, the teacher must be committed to intervene in socially charged, ethically challenging situations. And the collaboration doesn't always feel pleasant in the conventional, superficial sense of feeling good for the moment. It is a more profound definition of pleasantness that gratifies us not because it always leaves us feeling good, but because it affirms our struggle toward goodness.

When we intervene we intend to question, to identify the discomfort, to uncover the joint work we need to undertake. We do not intend to threaten or to blame. An example from several years ago comes to mind. I was teaching a literature class, discussing a passage in *I Know Why the Caged Bird Sings*, when we stopped to figure out a word. Victor's hand shot up, an unusual happening. He read off a fine definition when I noticed, from the corner of my eye, Josie and Liz snickering. I went on dissecting the passage, and then realized that I was preoccupied with the backdrop of events. I stopped the class, announced that I was upset, that I didn't understand the snickers. Josie, quick to explain, said she was laughing because Victor had clearly started his homework already. Now Victor was slow and easily confused. I was aware that he was often a mark, a target of unkind teasing, and not just from Josie, who was quick, blunt and impulsive. Liz chimed in, backing up Josie's explanation, and Victor began to apologize, to rationalize his work.

"Stop!" I almost yelled. I didn't want Victor apologizing. I didn't want Josie weaseling out of this either. I announced that it seemed terrific to me that people started assignments early and that I was bothered by the need to defend oneself in the group. "Why," I asked, "do people feel the need to be defensive?"

"Because they feel threatened?" ventured Justin.

"How is it that we have become a group where people feel threatened?" I asked. By that time I believe both Josie and Victor were crying. And we were off on perhaps the best social discussion, in its honest exploration of difficult issues, that year. It was not a topic that offered simple answers. Like all the case studies here, there were many knotted threads including sarcasm and teasing as verbal play, and the many reasons that children become marginal members of a group.

Sometimes when the children are volatile, unpredictable, hard to understand, their peers pull back.

In the adolescent community of my classroom overt cruelty is rare, but exclusion is not. Some children are never invited to sleepovers or movie trips, or enfolded into the comfortable chatter and play of the day. I have observed transfer students who, upon entering our school, are at first relieved that the taunts and bullying they had been subjected to in former settings is gone, but then saddened as they realize that they are still "outside." I am aware that this is detrimental to our community. I do not know the solution. I do know that I want to engage with the children in a struggle toward some answers in a "pleasant collaboration" in which I am ever mindful of my role and responsibilities as ethical coach.

CHAPTER TEN

COMMON PROBLEMS

"Why do they persist in this behavior even after we have talked and talked?" · "What does it mean that in front of me the children do one thing and behind my back they do the opposite?" · "Why isn't he working? Why do I have to keep pushing, prodding, nudging?" · "How do I get these children to really talk? Not just to say 'fine' and 'I like it'?"

Midway through, as I was reading all of the cases, I became aware that despite all the differences—different locations, different communities, different cultures, and different age-levels—there were some striking similarities. The particular case problems seemed to uncover what may be over-arching problems. Are there, in fact, a few general or universal problems which underlie teaching a social curriculum? I did find myself lumping together many different questions into six categories. Obviously from such a small sampling, it is rash to make too many assumptions. The themes that we identified are offered here as suggestions and as ways to help appreciate the connected layers of social teaching. To suggest that there may be broad categories of problems, which have many different particular questions and manifestations, is useful if it helps us to recognize and understand effective teaching methods centered around the work of the social curriculum. And if by linking an individual case with others we discover common ground and gain insight and encouragement, we may find much needed knowledge and support.

These themes also identify the critical goals of a social curriculum. Earlier in the project, the goals were expressed as conflicting tendencies. We wondered how children move, for example, from ritual to real learning or from external to internal controls. In the course of this work, a different goal emerged—the idea of finding a balance between different competing tendencies. Certainly one of the challenging aspects of teaching is the need to allow for so many differences in learning style, in rate of skill acquisition, in temperamental variation and approach. A synthesis of approaches is so often more effective than an either/or position. As I stated in my commentary on Colette Kaplan's study of boredom, there are times when children need rote and routine tasks. They need to memorize the times tables, state capitals or which way the cursive letters slant. They do not need to invent or create the answers. There are other times when imaginative and constructive responses are essential. The balance of right/wrong activities with open-ended and interpretive ones is often what allows a healthy flow of mental energy.

When my children were small, I remember reading with great relief that a balanced diet did not mean three helpings of food group one and two helpings of food group two for each and every meal. Instead, it was pointed out that sometimes children seem to want starches and other times proteins, the balance achieved over time rather than from each meal. Finding a balance of classroom emphasis may also need to be considered over time rather than day by day. When the tone feels off that may signal a time to reshift priorities. By balance, then, I suggest that both sides of a thematic equation are critical to the well-being of the program. And both sides must be sustained and integrated into the thoughtful management of classroom life.

The six suggested common "thematic" problems are

1. The balance between ritual and real
2. The balance between student-initiated and teacher-initiated learning
3. The balance between external controls and inner controls
4. The balance between individual and community needs
5. The balance between the academic and the social curriculum
6. The balance between common developmental goals and diversity

RITUAL AND REAL BEHAVIOR

Rituals provide ceremony, meaning, predictability, and continuity to our lives. We must, however, ensure that our rituals remain vital and personally meaningful and that their details continue to convey the spirit intended by the ceremony or routine. Meaningful rituals, when we really understand and participate in them, can infuse the spontaneous and less structured parts of our lives. I think of Jason, in Eileen's classroom, who literally steps out of the Greeting Circle in his class-room to offer his hand and a smile to a visitor in the doorway. The rit-ual has inserted itself into a situation in his classroom life.

Ritual and real, in an intricate weave, are part of our curriculum. We look at the situations in our classrooms to measure what is being learned from the procedures and lessons and rituals we teach. And, in return, our rituals often evolve from the instruction and observation of our day to day practice. Do the children go through the motions of conflict resolution but seethe underneath as Arona questions? As I ob-serve my students, so adept at the ritual of greeting, and often so neg-ligent in the spontaneous communications, I realize that I have some work to do.

Classroom teacher Steven Levy comments in *Starting from Scratch*, "Our character is the sum of our habits. It has to do with our most basic modes of perception and expression. It is not learned like facts in geography or science. Habits that form character are only estab-lished through repeated and continuous practice. They are not things one thinks are good ideas and adopts. They become part of the very fabric of one's being; they become automatic dispositions and re-sponses." (Levy, 1996, p. 155) Like most important learning, this does not usually happen quickly or smoothly. It often involves what Dottie explains to her students as the discomfort accompanying the learning curve. It often happens in small increments. "I know I'm mean," Richie boasts at the start of the year, " 'cause those kids are jerks. I hate them." Months later he softens the statement. He didn't intend to be really mean, "just joking." And slowly, sometimes through difficult ex-changes, in the meetings and greetings and sharings of the classroom, he is listening and getting to know "the jerks" better. Importantly, he is identifying with the desire for a more friendly and trustful class. "Well, I don't actually hate her."

Rituals offer a sense of expectation, an opportunity for repeated practice and a community culture. They provide a chance for children to begin to form habits—habits of greeting, of attention, of listening, of honest discussion, of work and effort, self-reliance, interest, affec-tion, and caring—what we have called in this project "habits of good-ness." The balance of ritual and real is revealed in the old adage,

"Character is what you do when no one is looking." We envision a synergy of ritual and real in which the ritual is not fake and the real is not unpracticed.

STUDENT-INITIATED AND TEACHER-INITIATED LEARNING

Teachers long to see their students engaged, self-motivated and excited to learn. We want to see active learners, interested in their work, eagerly revising, extending and doing. Often we do see our students in just this way. We also, however, can envision our dawdlers or slackers, passively awaiting, even dodging, our directives. We recall Colette's "bored" fifth graders, frittering away time because their teepee was "done."

Colette and many of the teachers in this project make frequent use of "choice," a structure that encourages active participation. As Dottie writes toward the end of her case, "Active participation grows when it can be concretely practiced within the confines of the room." Colette's class chooses roles in their work on the log cabin; they choose topics for maritime projects. They choose how they wish to represent the project, and they make choices about the extent of their investment. We see Dottie's class begin to make choices about their room design as well as choices also related to academic topics. Such choices certainly can empower students and give purpose and energy to their work.

But all the empowerment, all the opportunities to choose, all the stimulating and relevant projects will not ensure that every student is engaged and motivated to learn. We see, in Colette's class's log cabin project, an activity that almost all are wildly enthusiastic about, a few who still do not engage. At first, Dottie's room plans seem to interest only a few. Individual frustrations and fears can distance children.

When this happens we see teachers inventing and inserting structures which help children become involved. Colette limits the options for her reluctant builder. "You may do this or this," she says. Unspoken but powerful is the implication: you will do. Both Colette and Dottie find formats for critique and discussion which encourage children to learn from each other in systematic, supportive ways. Structures and expectations that teachers create, along with a generous amount of room for choice within those structures and expectations, will help children learn to make and enjoy productive choices.

External Controls and Inner Controls

"To simply remove external controls, is not to create inner ones. It is more likely that we leave children prey to the tyranny of impulse."
—John Dewey

I do not view external and inner controls as polar opposites. Nor do I believe that getting older is a simple process of going from outer to inner controls. To be sure, as we get older we rely more on our inner controls. Ideally, we have a code of ethics and social knowledge to draw on and refer to though we all know the powers of temptation and persuasion that urge us to consume, to leap the railings, to exceed the speed limits. The struggle between impulse and rationality and between gratification and ethics is an ongoing plot. It is key to the quest for a moral and ethical life. Our task is to give students the tools and the appetite to embrace this struggle. Thus, the two-pronged task involves first teaching students to care about the struggle to acquire social skills and ethical understanding and then teaching them how to act to use those skills in ethical ways. Finding the proper balance between limit-setting and self-governance at each developmental stage is the challenge. What are the incremental steps of privilege and trust?

Individual and Community Needs

"I want all the blocks."
"But in school we share."
"I need them all."

How do we balance individual needs and community needs? When is it important for the individual's needs to be second to the community's needs? When is it important to acknowledge and honor individual differences and variables? Fairness is not necessarily treating everyone the same, I believe. Fairness in school may be when people get what they most need. Micky needs to bring a ball of clay to the meeting rug to help his hands stay in control . . . but the rest of us don't. That's OK.

The Academic Curriculum and Social Curriculum

In Cathy's study, Jack understands the impact of his teasing when he listens to a beautifully expressed, carefully edited and final-drafted piece of writing from a classmate. A student in Colette's class wants to revise his work when he observes the results of superior efforts by his peers. Arona extends her children's ability to understand sharing using

reading and writing. The academic skills of making books, recording problems, and increasing vocabulary are integrated seamlessly into social problem-solving. Similarly, Dottie infuses and broadens the academic challenges of American history and Greek culture with concrete applications to classroom dilemmas. We see times when a challenging academic task is a springboard for social growth and times when the social intricacies and questions of a group inspire academic learning.

I am reminded of a question posed to me recently when I was making a presentation on the social curriculum at a Lesley College conference. The group was in the midst of an interesting, lively discussion about how children decide on partners when a reporter asked, "If you spend all this time on choosing partners, when do you ever teach content?"

Good question. There is an unfortunate tendency in this country to swing back and forth between polarized trends: process vs. content; back-to-basics vs. integrated learning; whole language vs. phonics; and social vs. academic curriculum. Any good approach must achieve synthesis and balance. We want children to know how to use a dictionary, write effectively, and make change in a supermarket. We also want children to care about themselves, each other, and their environment. We want them to grow into adults who care about water quality in our rivers and housing quality in our cities, and who have the knowledge and drive to make improvements. As I hope our case studies illustrate, these are mutually inclusive, not exclusive, goals.

COMMON DEVELOPMENTAL GOALS AND DIVERSITY

The issue of diversity influenced, at least in part, Arona McNeill-Vann's case study. Questions certainly have been raised about the implications of certain teaching practice for non-middle class children and students of color. If I understand the arguments put forth by educators such as Lisa Delpit, adaptations of commonly accepted progressive practices are usually made in the name of remediation and deficit reduction. Delpit advocates a very different perspective. In *Other People's Children*, she writes, "It is time to look closely at elements of our educational system . . . time to see whether there is minority involvement and support, and if not, to ask why." (Delpit, 1995, p. 10) I do not think that Delpit, for one, is arguing against humanizing reforms in school. What she has questioned is whether instructional approaches, such as whole language, or writing process, enable African-American students to acquire the language skills they need to be successful in school. If not, do other approaches work better? Where is the educational dialogue that assesses the ability or failure of methods to reach across cultural lines?

If teachers are going to be better able to educate "other people's children," our teaching must be informed by knowledge of what best serves all children. This knowledge, I suspect, can emerge if dialogue replaces polarization. We must continue to seek out ways to make our schools a place where all children can and do learn. How do we best do that?

IN SUMMARY

The case studies presented here grew out of problems chosen by teachers, problems that had created some disequilibrium, some sense of uneasiness in the teachers' own classrooms. We built a case study process using a number of standard elements but kept it flexible enough to fit the design of inservice teaching. We have tried to highlight those parts of the process that best encourage problem-solving over an extended period of time, in collaboration with others, with both short and long-term results. Teachers were not asked to come up with a final solution. Instead they looked at those things that worked along the way. Interestingly, even those teachers who worked on their cases for most of a year wanted more time and raised more questions in the end than the beginning. Fortunately, there is always next year!

Chapter Eleven

REFLECTIVE PRACTICE
A Conclusion of Sorts

We started with the story of "habits of goodness." It is a way we have come to view the task of teaching the social curriculum, a way to encourage a yearning to care for ourselves, each other and our world. We recognize that we bring the teaching of habits of goodness into the heart of classroom activity by the rituals and structures we invent and by our moments of notice and intervention.

As I was sifting through my case study files, I uncovered a letter I had written to Linda Mathews midway through the project. In a piece of writing she had sent me titled "Reflections," she had written of a workshop she attended where she was told that classroom teachers make 2,000 to 7,000 split-second decisions every single day. I responded:

> Now I know why I am so loathe to even think about what we should have for dinner tonight. My decision-making cells are burnt out! Humor aside, it is so true that teachers wrestle continuously with decisions and questions, often alone. Your recent enclosure titled "Reflections" struck me, perhaps because it seemed an odd combo—teaching and reflections. Reflections make me think of bubble baths and long sits by the ocean. I think about stillness and quiet. I never think about the hectic pace, the combustion and kaleidoscope of the classroom. Yet to reflect is the aim of our case studies. It is the ideal, what we hope to accomplish—to sit back, to compose ourselves, to look at the reflections of our classroom ponds so that we can be reflective.
>
> Still intrigued by this word, I have looked it up in my Webster's dictionary. Reflect: to throw or bend back (heat, light, sound) from a surface. Perhaps that is it really—to let the sounds, the light, the heads of the children, the surface sensations of school life be re-seen, re-imaged, to bend yet again into new understandings.

A reflection from my own classroom life forms itself in my mind's eye. It is the first week of school. My co-teachers and I have taken the class out to play a rousing game of tag. The children look forward to these organized break times. Fun, we tell them, means that the play is safe and enjoyable for everyone. Today does not start well. There are grumbles about the choice of game. A shove and an underhanded comment. We stop the game. "I'm noticing that this is not fun and safe for everyone," I say. "What do you notice?" The observations are quick and honest. We will return to the classroom and try again later or to-morrow. Eventually, we will be able to play as a group with gusto and reasonable limits. We will have fun. Eventually the older children will manage their own games and even coach the younger. We will hear our own words echoing across the playground: "It has to be fun for everyone," twelve-year-old Julie and Mike will remind their seven-year-old charges. Of course there will be those times, too, when the older ones forget or defy, bully or sulk. And we will try to remember that habits are not frozen solid, but are evolving dispositions to con-tinually interpret and construct.

Sometimes I fear that we will lose faith, faith in ourselves and our children. Many teachers find their classes harder, their children demonstrating fewer academic and social skills. In my school, too, the challenges can be daunting. More than ever we need to feel the courage and hope of our profession. We need the time and stamina to problem-solve, to search in our own midst for effective strategies and to collaborate in interesting and pleasant conversations.

Our teaching life—filled with our children and our classrooms—refuses to stay still. It churns, roils and rushes, and every so often it sparkles with light and beauty. What does reflective practice have to do with the reality of the classroom then? As we reflect, we are better able to accept the nature of our struggles and to find the problems of our classroom invitations to learn. And perhaps even more signifi-cantly, as we take on these invitations, as we dignify this struggle, we are better able to ally ourselves with the children, the parents, the com-munity and one another to construct a future that has hope. It is a hope that must, in some measure, come from teachers watching the spill grow, urging on and wondering aloud about the latest play fight, encouraging real talk, and sharing that comes from underneath.

APPENDIX
Case Study Outline

Writers of case studies should select a problem that truly engages them and has an impact on their own work. The problem should be current, interesting and 'ripe for the pickin!' Problems may be specific and concrete: awful recess times; sneaky, secretive behavior among 5th grade girls, etc. Or problems may be broader in their initial conception: self-control issues in middle grades; poor listening skills; low levels of trust, etc. It is important that the problems chosen do not come with ready-made answers and that teachers are clear about their preconceptions. It is important to be willing to tackle, research, grope around and to raise questions that we may not be able to answer yet.

I.   Summary of school/classroom background and context: Describe demographics.

II. Initial description of problem(s): Define problem and state reasons for teacher concern.

III. Description of teacher/writer: Describe why you selected this particular case to study. Try to identify your own opinions, assumptions, "personal filters" (button-pushers and convictions).

IV. Observations (2–3) of problem: Gather these over a week or two as a basis for observation and naming the behaviors and incidents which will be studied.

V.   Restatement of the problem after observations
     A. Describe problem to be studied
     B. Identify developmental characteristics related to the problem
     C. Anticipate behaviors and difficulties

VI. Statement of "Clear Positives"
     A. Frame objectives into positive challenges and desired behaviors for class. Break down global statements such as "efficient transitions" into clear expectations and definitions. Does "efficient" mean ten minutes or three?
     B. Include in each objective ways to identify and measure success. (Teacher and students need to monitor and mark progress. Ways to recognize and celebrate work in progress and completions need to be specific and clearly communicated.)
     C. State how parents and other staff members will be involved.

VII. Methods of observation (How study will be conducted)
    A. Make direct observations and keep anecdotal records.
    B. Tape discussions.
    C. Have conferences with colleagues.
    D. Collect observations from students.
    E. Note reflections and readings.

VIII. Action plan: Strategies and interventions for change
    A. Describe interventions
       1. Role-play
       2. Modeling
       3. Discussions
       4. Directed projects, etc.
    B. Describe methods of encouragement and measures of progress
       1. Class discussions
       2. Class writing
       3. Observation recordings
       4. Criteria for change
    C. Record reflections and results
       1. Student reflections
       2. Teacher reflections
       3. Collegial/editorial reflections

IX.   Conferencing
Each case study writer will have a conferencing partner to share experiences and ideas and to revise and enhance the critique process. The opportunity for critical reflection will be central to the case study method. Conferences include:
    A. Anecdotal and journal entries
    B. Shared observations
    C. Suggestions for new or revised strategies
    D. Failures and successes

X.   Results and Conclusions
    A. What important questions have been raised?
    B. What has worked/not worked?
    C. What structural and program changes have you made?
    D. What did you learn from this case study?
    E. What do you feel the children learned?
    F. What are the implications for your classroom/school/self/next year?

NOTES

1 My re-telling of this story derives from Hallie's speech—as I remember it. After the draft of this manuscript was completed, I discovered that Hallie had written a book recounting this story in far more detail and complexity. Readers who are interested will find the book fascinating: *Lest Innocent Blood Be Shed* by Phillip Hallie (New York: Harper & Row, 1979).

2 *The Responsive Classroom,*® created by Northeast Foundation for Children, is a collection of teaching strategies designed to help elementary school teachers integrate the teaching of both social and academic skills through their daily classroom management and academic approaches.

3 My understanding of Berger's ideas about critiquing comes primarily from a workshop he led for Greenfield Center School staff in the spring of 1996.

REFERENCES

Adande, J. A. 1996. Iverson Will Remain in School, Coach Says. *The Washington Post*, March 5.

Baldwin, James. 1955. *Notes of a Native Son*. Boston, Massachusetts: Beacon Press.

Benard, Cheryl. 1996. Mediation Minus Morals. *The Washington Post*, February 25.

Canada, Geoffrey. 1995. *Fist, Stick, Knife, Gun: A Personal History of Violence in America*. Boston, Massachusetts: Beacon Press.

Carnegie Report. 1996. "Years of Promise." Report of Carnegie Task Force on Learning in Primary Grades. New York: Carnegie Corporation of New York.

Charney, Ruth. 1992. *Teaching Children to Care*. Greenfield, Massachusetts: NEFC.

Delpit, Lisa. 1995. *Other People's Children. Cultural Conflict in the Classroom*. New York: The New Press.

Dewey, John. 1938. *Experience and Education*. London: MacMillan.

Doris, Ellen. 1991. *Doing What Scientists Do*. Portsmouth, New Hampshire: Heinemann.

Dorris, Michael. 1994. *Guests*. New York: Hyperion.

Duckworth, Eleanor. 1987. *"The Having of Wonderful Ideas" and Other Essays on Teaching and Learning*. New York: Teachers College Press.

Faber, Adele and Elaine Mazlish. 1982. *How To Talk So Kids Will Listen & Listen So Kids Will Talk*. New York: Avon.

Hallie, Phillip. 1979. *Lest Innocent Blood Be Shed*. New York: Harper & Row.

Handford, Martin. 1987. *Where's Waldo?* Boston, Massachusetts: Little, Brown & Company.

Heilbrun, Carolyn G. 1988. *Writing a Woman's Life*. New York: Ballantine Books.

High Scope Educational Research Foundation. *The Cognitively Oriented Curriculum*. Ypsilanti, Michigan: The High Scope Press.

Levy, Steven. 1996. *Starting From Scratch*. Portsmouth, New Hampshire: Heinemann.

Maslow, Abraham. 1970. *Motivation and Personality*. New York: Harper & Row.

Mayer, Mercer. 1992. *When I Get Mad*. Racine, Wisconsin: Western Publishing, Co.

McDermott, Gerald. 1987. *Anansi The Spider: A Tale from the Ashanti*. New York: H. Holt and Co.

Meier, Deborah. 1995. *The Power of Their Ideas*. Boston, Massachusetts: Beacon Press.

Noddings, Nel. 1984. *Caring: A Feminine Approach to Ethics & Moral Education.* Berkeley, California: University of California Press.

Paley, Vivian. 1992. *You Can't Say You Can't Play.* Cambridge, Massachusetts: Harvard University Press.

Piaget, Jean. 1965. *The Moral Judgment of the Child.* New York: The Free Press.

Pipher, Mary. 1996. *The Shelter of Each Other.* New York: Putnam.

Ruddick, Sara. 1989. *Maternal Thinking: Toward a Politics of Peace.* Boston, Massachusetts: Beacon Press.

Strachota, Bob. 1996. *On Their Side.* Greenfield, Massachusetts: NEFC.

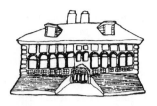

Northeast Foundation for Children

RESOURCES FOR TEACHERS

Since 1985, Northeast Foundation for Children
has published books on education for those
who believe in the importance
of developmentally appropriate practices
and a strong social curriculum in our schools.
In addition to its publishing activities,
Northeast Foundation for Children offers
educational workshops and consulting services
and operates Greenfield Center School,
a K–8 school in Greenfield, Massachusetts.

Additionally, NEFC publishes a newsletter,
The Responsive Classroom: A Newsletter for Teachers,
which is mailed three times each year
to educators nationwide. Subscriptions are free.
Please call or write to be added to the mailing list.

Teaching Children to Care: Management in the Responsive Classroom
by Ruth Sidney Charney

Speaking to the heart of every classroom teacher, this 314-page book offers a proven, practical approach that helps reduce the exhausting and often overwhelming classroom management problems confronting today's K–8th grade teachers. *Teaching Children to Care* presents theory, practical guidelines, and real-life examples which show how to create classrooms where caring is practiced.

Habits of Goodness: Case Studies in the Social Curriculum
by Ruth Sidney Charney

Six experienced public school teachers present case studies in which they think about and work to resolve problems in their classrooms. Ruth Charney, best-selling author of *Teaching Children to Care*, presents commentary on each case, explores classroom management practices, reflects upon the process of problem solving in teachers' professional development, and highlights universal themes which emerge from these case studies.

Yardsticks: Children in the Classroom, Ages 4–14
by Chip Wood

This user-friendly guidebook helps teachers and parents to better understand children by offering clear and concise descriptions of developmental characteristics of each age. Each description is followed by charts with developmental "yardsticks" in the areas of physical, social, language, and cognitive growth. Also included in this 228-page book are curriculum guidelines and a list of favorite books for different ages.

On Their Side: Helping Children Take Charge of Their Learning
by Bob Strachota

Written in a personal voice, full of warmth, humor and honesty, the author shares his many effective strategies for helping to create classrooms where children really care about and take responsibility for their learning and behavior. In just 160 pages, Bob Strachota shows how to ally with children, how to ask questions which engage children in real learning, and how to share power with students while also enforcing high standards. Powerful reading for new and experienced teachers alike.

A Notebook for Teachers: Making Changes in the Elementary Curriculum
by Northeast Foundation for Children Staff

This timeless resource can help teachers integrate developmentally appropriate teaching techniques into the classroom. *A Notebook for Teachers* includes details on the behavior characteristics of 5, 6 and 7-year olds, as well as classroom implications. This 79-page guide includes over 150 charts, examples, photographs and illustrations.

Places to Start: Implementing the Developmental Classroom
Written, Photographed & Presented by Marlynn K. Clayton

This 90-minute classic in the field of developmentally appropriate practices provides a wealth of practical, effective ideas that have been classroom tested over many years. These ideas work to create an active, productive, learning and caring classroom community. From NEFC's acclaimed workshop slideshow. Includes 25-page viewing guide.

For Ordering Information

Publishing Division
NEFC
71 Montague City Rd.
Greenfield, MA 01301

phone: 800-360-6332
fax: 413-772-2097
www.responsiveclassroom.org